NEVERSINK

READING'S "OTHER" MOUNTAIN

(THE RESORT YEARS: 1880-1930)

BY PAUL A. DRUZBA

EXETER HOUSE BOOKS
2003

Neversink: Reading's "Other" Mountain
(The Resort Years: 1880-1930)

by Paul A. Druzba

©2003 Paul A. Druzba
ISBN: 1-880683-18-0

All Rights Reserved. No portion of this book may be reproduced in any form without written permission from the owner of this copyright.
Printed in the United States of America

Table of Contents

Introduction
    page 5

Map of Neversink & the Railway
    page 10-11

Part 1- Facts and Figures
    page 12

Part 2- Native Americans
    page 16

Part 3- Transportation and Neversink
    page 21

Part 4- A Place To Relax
    page 26

Part 5- The Neversink Mountain Railroad
    page 29

Part 6- The Resorts
    page 60

Chapter 1- The White House
           The First Resort
    page 61

Chapter 2- The Highland House
    page 70

Chapter 3- Haak Farm/Quarry
    page 86

Chapter 4- Hiener's Wissel
    page 91

Chapter 5- Neversink Mountain Hotel
    page 95

Chapter 6- Centennial Springs Hotel/
    Berks County Tuberculosis Sanatorium
    page 117

Chapter 7- Point Lookout
    page 134

Chapter 8- Klapperthal Area
    page 137

Chapter 9- Klapperthal Park Station
    page 140

Chapter 10- Klapperthal Pavilion/
    Klapperthal Station
    page 144

Chapter 11- Dengler's Glen Hotel/
    The Last Resort?
    Page 155

Part 7- Random Notes
    page 166

Part 8- Traces & A Look Ahead
    page 180

Introduction

Over the years, Mount Penn has enjoyed the lion's share of the attention in most historical and promotional accounts of Reading, Pa. and Berks County, thanks to its being the site of that icon of Berks- the Pagoda. Much has been written about both Mount Penn and its famous landmark.

But there is another mountain that flanks east Reading which has an equally interesting history in its own right- Neversink.

This relatively overlooked mountain wasn't always so- it saw a flurry of development that occurred on its peaks and valleys in the late Nineteenth and early Twentieth Centuries.

In fact, even though Neversink is a bit shorter than Mount Penn in stature, the size and scale of commercial enterprise during Neversink's salad days dwarfed those on Mount Penn during a period which could be called "The Resort Years," from 1880 through 1930, due primarily to the strategic location of Neversink Mountain, relative to the Schuylkill River and the Philadelphia and Reading Railroad.

Still, in the 21st Century, it's a classic case of "out of sight, out of mind." Only one small structure still remains on Neversink from the "old days-" the McIlvain Pavilion- and you would need a telescope to see it from Reading.

5

In 1959, a Reading Eagle reporter had the nerve to refer to Neversink as "Mount Penn's shabbier, smaller sister to the south." Smaller? Yes. But "shabbier"? And J. Earl Ruthardt, in a very negative article on Neversink in the Reading Times in 1977, described Neversink as "rising dejectedly over the city." If it seems that I'm writing this with an attitude, I am. I'm from east Reading, I'm proud of Neversink, and I think the mountain is due a little respect. In fact, OVERdue.

The Schuylkill Canal and the railroad are often cited as being the catalysts for growth in Reading. Although the Philadelphia and Reading Railroad played a major role in the development of Neversink Mountain in the late 19th Century, at least some of the development was due not to the railroad, but rather to the instinct of individual entrepreneurs. So, while some of the resort attractions on Neversink had a common origin, each has its own story and players.

About the only thing that connected all of these independent enterprises during Neversink's boom period was the Neversink Mountain Railroad, which stopped at each in its heyday.

The "usual" way of telling a story is to tell it from beginning to end. And, while the story of Neversink's Resort Years begins early and ends late, it is not just one story, but many.

Telling the story of Neversink's Resort Period in a strictly chronological way would be very confusing, because many things were happening around the same time at various places on the mountain. So, to avoid constantly "jumping around" geographically, this narrative will "jump around" a bit in time.

Each of the attractions on Neversink, including the Neversink Mountain Railroad, will be dealt with as a story of its own, and in its entirety, from beginning to end. The Neversink Mountain Railroad's stops were not arranged on the mountain in order of when each attraction appeared- it was rather a geographic decision. (The White House Hotel was a well established landmark on Neversink well before the railway appeared, as was the Highland House; and the Neversink Mountain Hotel did not yet exist when the railroad was built.)

The "chapters" in Part 6, "The Resorts," will also be noted by "Stop Numbers," which correspond to a typical ticket for a ride on the Neversink Mountain Railway. The stop numbers are **based** on actual tickets, but include all stops throughout the railroad's history.

Taken as a whole then, this book can serve not only as a narrative of a unique period in Berks County history, but also as a "travel guide" for the hiker and history buff.

For comparison purposes, it's interesting to note that the Gravity Railroad on Mount Penn never stopped at the Pagoda, which is the only original landmark from that period which survives on Mount Penn to this day. Similarly, the Neversink Mountain Railroad was built before the Neversink Mountain Hotel existed. The difference was, the Neversink Mountain Hotel was a place where the Neversink railway would have wanted to stop. The Pagoda, though it now enjoys the status of "THE" landmark on Mount Penn, never enjoyed that status during the time the Mt. Penn Gravity Railroad existed.

Notes

History, if it is to live at all, cannot live in a vacuum. Events are sometimes influenced by or result in other lesser, seemingly unrelated events which add perspective to the larger event, or of the time in which it occurred.

So, that mouthful said, you will find notes of interest attached to many of the stories here which, hopefully, will add to your appreciation of this unique time in Berks County history. Think of them as a little salsa for the chips.

The resorts are covered roughly in the order in which they appeared, with a few exceptions. The most notable: The Neversink Mountain Hotel is covered sooner than it occurred. The reason is- it just makes a better story that way. The Neversink Mountain Hotel impacted other resorts, and telling the story of some of the others would not make sense without first telling the story of the "big one."

There were several instances where the evidence was contradictory. One was the location of the trolley station at Klapperthal Park. Some written evidence, as well as the memories of several people, stated that it was on the west side of the glen. But I have a photo that shows it clearly on the other side. Sorry- I have to go with the photo.

I have made every effort to be as factual and accurate as possible, and to avoid litigation; but I also tend to be rather opinionated and judgmental, and I make no apologies.

Ideally, research involves interviewing those who could tell the story. In my two years of research, I did that to the extent that I could, but virtually all of the people who would remember Neversink Mountain from this period are dead. And the memories of those still around are sometimes fuzzy.

Still, the experiences of people are what bring a story to life, and I've included as many of those as I could.

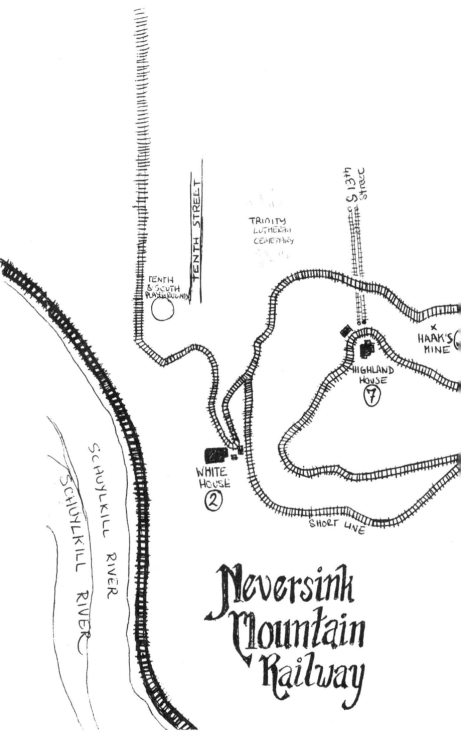

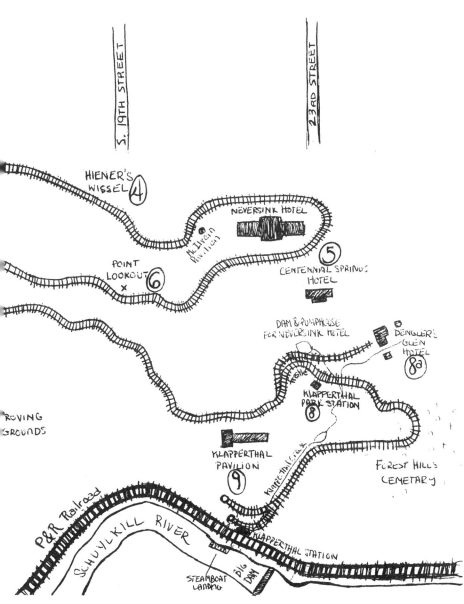

Part 1- Facts & Figures

Neversink Mountain is the first geologic elevation of any significance that one encounters traveling upstream from the mouth of the Schuylkill River at Philadelphia. It stretches for about two miles, rising gradually in Exeter Township, and ending suddenly, with steep slopes in east Reading, covering 1,352 acres.

The mountain falls under the jurisdiction of six municipalities- The City of Reading, Mount Penn Borough, St. Lawrence Borough, Lower Alsace Township, Cumru Township and Exeter Township.

Because of its orientation (west to east, from the perspective of Reading, as opposed to Mount Penn, which runs south to north), Neversink's climate and vegetation differ widely from one face to the other, and from the foothills to the peaks.

Vegetation along the base tends to be lush, with a predominance of deciduous trees. Near the top, evergreens are more common, and growth at the top is much slower than at the bottom. Temperatures at the top tend to be more extreme- higher in the summer than the bottom, and lower in the winter. Naturally, snow melts a lot faster on the south face, making sledding a more viable option on the north side (several sledding trips in my youth confirm this.)

During the "mid seasons-" spring and fall- the hiker is advised to "layer" clothing. Temperatures, especially at higher elevations, can change substantially within just a few hundred yards. The shirtsleeves that seemed comfortable at the glen may cause goose bumps at the western peak.

The lush vegetation at the bottom is due at least in part to the very porous soil on the mountain. You'll find very few streams on Neversink, and some of these appear from and disappear into "nowhere.". Visible streams (e.g.- Hiener's Spring and Klapperthal Creek) are common at lower elevations, and the surface water promotes more lush growth.

This extreme porosity and lack of groundwater at higher elevations has been a major impediment to fire fighting on the mountain, at least in theory, and most of the fires that destroyed the major resorts on Neversink were at the peaks. But in all fairness to Mother Nature, none of these fires can be easily attributable to natural causes.

In terms of the mountain itself, many damaging fires have also occurred at lower elevations, but these have been due more to the railroad than to the nature of the mountain.

The seasons also arrive and depart at different times at different places on Neversink, depending on the elevation. Spring arrives early at Klapperthal Glen on the south side and eastern end of the mountain, and about three weeks later up the face from Klapperthal, at the eastern peak.

According to local authorities on flora and fauna, Neversink is home to two species of endangered butterflies, and to uncommon ferns and moss in the Klapperthal area.

The highest peak of Neversink, the eastern peak, is 903 feet above sea level. (This compares to Mount Penn, which reaches 1,250 feet, and contradicts several published estimates of Neversink's height to be as high as 1,000 feet.)

The geology of Neversink is also a little unusual. Contrary to what you'll normally see on a mountain, the rock formations at lower levels of Klapperthal Glen are actually newer, being a gray limestone which was washed in from the north. This happened when the African plate collided with the North American plate, and formed the Appalachian Mountains. Farther uphill, you'll see red sandstone, which is the older formation.

Though Neversink is now covered with a thick layer of vegetation, it wasn't always so. Until about the middle of the 20th Century, residents of the surrounding communities used Neversink as a source of firewood and building materials. In fact, in the 1930's, workers with the Works Progress Administration (WPA) were paid 10 cents an hour to cut trees on Neversink. Logging trails are still in evidence in a number of locations. So the Neversink you see today has only been enjoying relatively undisturbed growth on its surface (except for fires) for about 50 years.

The mountain has also been used for a quarry operation, a reservoir, a testing ground for cannon during the Civil War, as a landfill, for farming, and as a source of minerals for paint manufacture.

But we're getting ahead of ourselves. No history of Neversink Mountain would be complete without at least a mention of the people who first enjoyed the bounty which once was available on and around the mountain.

The flag of the Lenni Lenape tribe of the Delaware. This is a modern day concoction. The 18th Century Lenni Lenape had no concept of flags, but it IS representative of who they were.

Part 2- Native Americans

An English corruption of the Lenni Lenape word "navasink," which means "on the promontory," Neversink Mountain takes its name from these first visitors to Berks County's "horseshoe curve" in the Schuylkill River. Neversink actually did have a very impressive promontory at one time, which was referred to as "Lover's Leap." But this story has more to do with the railroad than it does with the Lenni Lenape, so we'll talk about that later.

Note: "Navasink" is often translated in existing narratives as "the fishing place," but this is incorrect, according to several Lenni-Lenape/Delaware dictionaries and phrase books. It is also illogical. One would not refer to a mountain as a "fishing place" unless there were a lake on top. The banks along the Schuylkill could be referred to as their "fishing place," but if the Lenni Lenape had a word that meant "fishing place," I haven't heard it. It certainly was not "navasink."

The Unami clan of the Lenni Lenape (len-ah'-pay) tribe originated in what is now New Jersey and Delaware. Their origin explains why the 21st Century remnants of the tribe are often referred to as "The Delaware."

Some modern-day members of the tribe look on the term "Lenni Lenape" as redundant. "Lenape" in the Delaware language, means "common people."

"Lenni Lenape," according to 21st Century Delaware, would mean "common, common people." But let's not be picky.

Speaking of semantics, the "Schuylkill River" was known to the Lenni Lenape as "manayunk," which means "where we drink," but that's a name which would be adopted by a community about 40 miles down river, just west of Philadelphia.

The Lenni Lenape tribe's banner (flag) shows the three clans of the tribe. The "Unami," which inhabited the Berks region, designated by a turtle; the "Monsey" clan, represented by a wolf print; and the "Unalachtgos" clan, represented by a turkey claw.

The tribe's peaceful nature is also symbolized by a peace pipe and fire starter in front of a mask. Rounding out the symbols on the flag is a Christian cross at the top, reflecting the influence of the Europeans they would eventually encounter in their travels.
The Unami clan was the most powerful in the tribe, and presided over all of their meetings, which were held in Shackamaxon.

Since the Lenni Lenape were initially migratory, they had no real "home" in the Berks County area until about 1700, when the white settlers from Europe began to arrive. That's when their lifestyle changed from migration to agriculture, which dictated a more stationery lifestyle.

If you're interested in searching for arrowheads or other artifacts, you'll do better sticking to the banks of the Schuylkill River. The Lenni Lenape found a wealth of shad in the Schuylkill River, and plenty of game along its banks. So they never found the need to wander far uphill. As one local Neversink authority pointed out from the top of the mountain, "They wouldn't be stupid enough to climb up here- all the food was down there."

Just as the Lenni Lenape were "settling down" in the Reading area, however, they were being squeezed out by other "settlers" in the region- the Swedes, the Germans and the Dutch.

The new European settlers put pressure on the Lenni Lenape to move north- the only place where they could go to escape the spread of white encroachment onto their native lands.

Although there was some inter-marriage between the Lenape and the white settlers, by 1730 the Lenni Lenape were basically gone from the Reading area, on their way north to their eventual homeland- the Chatham, Ontario area of Canada.

Other than providing shad, deer and wild turkey for the Lenni Lenape, and lumber for construction of Reading homes, Neversink Mountain has only a geological history until the arrival of the next "settlers" in the 1830s- the coal carriers.

A Lenni Lenape Chief removes a youngster's arrowhead from a successfully hunted buck. From a 1938 book on the Lenni Lenape. (Illustration: Clarence Ellsworth)

Typical Lenape garb, presumably the colder weather variety. The woman's clothing especially would have been unbearable on an August afternoon on Neversink.

Part 3- Transportation and Neversink

By around 1820, when the only Lenni Lenape left in the Berks County area were those who had mingled and married into white culture, the Schuylkill Canal was being built, linking Reading (and the nearby coal fields to the north) with Philadelphia. Canal boats were wading over what was left of the shad on which the Lenni Lenape had subsisted.

Problems on both ends were teaming up to destroy the fishing and the quality of the water in the river. Coal silt was collecting in the river and on the canals from the coal mining and industrial activities upstream.

But, down river on the outskirts of Philadelphia, the Fairmount Water Works had been created in 1819, and the accompanying dam blocked the shad's spawning route upriver. So even if the coal dust didn't do them in, their way would have been blocked by the dam. Nowadays, we have environmental impact studies.

The canal system was soon expanded and improved, and traffic on the canals and river increased.

By the way, when the Schuylkill Canal was being dug, human skeletons were dug up in the process, just east of the "Big Dam" at Klapperthal, indicating that this had been a burial place for the Native American inhabitants. Today, construction would be stopped for archeological study. But in the early 1800s, the attitude was- "that's interesting, but let's keep digging." At least they noticed.

The canals were a method of cheap transportation. And they were fueling a growth in the population of Reading, which would soon explode with the arrival of another, even cheaper form of transportation.

The Philadelphia and Reading Railroad was incorporated in 1833, and the line from Reading to Philadelphia was opened in 1839. Soon after, the line was hauling coal from the fields above Reading to Port Richmond in Philadelphia.

The railroad could deliver goods cheaper, faster and more reliably than the canals, which tended to freeze up in winter, dry out in summer, and were relatively slow. How slow were the canals? Picture a mule pulling a tractor-trailer.

Though the Philadelphia and Reading Railroad's headquarters was initially in Philadelphia, its power base was shifting more and more to Reading- the center of the company's activities. By the 1870s, the P&R railroad expanded into a corporate giant- the largest corporation in the world- whose operations included coal mining, iron making, canal and sea-going transportation, even shipbuilding. (Eventually, in 1925, the name "Philadelphia" would be dropped from the name, and the railroad would become known as "The Reading Company".)

In addition to all of its "industrial" cargo, the railroad was also making it possible for human cargo to quickly and easily make the journey from Reading to Philadelphia, or vice versa. People in Philadelphia could now visit the relatively "rural" Reading area, to escape the pressures and crowding of the "big city" down the Schuylkill.

As the railroad expanded northward, passengers and cargo from New York also began arriving in Reading. And the railroad, and the powers-that-be in Reading, would do what they thought necessary to make them feel at home.

Another form of transportation that would enhance the "Resort Years" of Neversink Mountain was the Reading trolley system.

Actually, in the mid 1800s, the Reading trolley system really wasn't much of a system at all. It was a hodgepodge of independent companies operating trolley lines in various parts of the city. These trolley lines continued to expand outward as the population grew. But a real system finally started to take shape in the late 1800s.

The Reading Traction Company was organized in 1893, and leased many of the city's scattered trolley lines, including extensions to the 9th and 10th Street lines, which had been laid in 1886.

Note: The railroads were a crucial part of daily life in the late 19th Century. The four-page daily Reading Eagle's front page was dominated every day by railroad news and schedules. It must be understood that the automobile was still at least 15 years in the future, and the railroads were how people and products got from place to place.

Car crashes in the 21st Century are a common occurrence; in the 1890s, the same could be said for train wrecks. It wasn't unusual for the *Reading Eagle* or the *Berks And Schuylkill Journal* to report a wreck that had killed 21 this day, or 10 the next, and these wrecks often did not even make it to the front page. They were a fact of life. There was a risk in day-to-day living, and train wrecks were considered an acceptable risk. Not that they were welcome.

A newspaper article from 1892 quoted figures from the Interstate Commerce Commission, noting that, of the 749,000 railroad employees in the United States the previous year, 2,451 had been killed.

Among those actually working aboard the trains, roughly one out of every 100 trainmen nationwide was killed each year, and one in twelve was injured. Most of the deaths occurred from falling from the train, or from mishaps in coupling. As a result, the ICC labeled railroading the most dangerous occupation in America- even worse than coal mining.

Today, if driving a car were an occupation, it would probably also be considered the most dangerous occupation in America. But, thanks to tougher safety standards, the automobile of today cannot claim to kill one of every 100 drivers per year.

Berks and Schuylkill Journal 1892

Part 4- A Place to Relax

Back in the early days of the Philadelphia and Reading Railroad, when Reading was upgraded in status from a borough to a city in 1848, the population was a mere 13,000. By 1898, it had grown to 73,000.*

That's a five-fold increase in only 50 years, thanks at least in part to the wealth and opportunity created by the railroad.

And thanks to the accessibility of Philadelphia to Reading residents, local papers like the *Reading Eagle* began to run more ads for Philadelphia businesses next to the ones by Reading merchants.

The residents of Reading, whose political persuasion was decidedly Democrat in the early 19th Century, began enjoying the financial benefits of the city's prosperity, and became more Republican in their politics by the turn of the 20th Century. (Ever heard the saying, "A Democrat is just a Republican with no money in his pocket?")

Readingites (Readingers?) also began to feel more cramped, and in need of open space in which to enjoy their free time.

They flocked to suburban sanctuaries, like Charles Evans Cemetery, a garden cemetery "outside" the city to the north, created in 1846.

Then, later in the century, to Penn's Common (which would take on the name of "City Park," when it was renovated at a then staggering cost of $6,000, from a sheep grazing spot into a "proper park.")

It's important to note that, from the 1830s until 1878, most of City Park was owned by the County of Berks, contrary to the wishes of Richard and Thomas Penn, who had designated the park as property of the "citizens of Reading" more than 100 years earlier.

The County, in cahoots with the Berks County Agricultural and Horticultural Society, had leased the park to the Society for the purpose of a once-a-year fair, and the grounds were inaccessible to the citizens of Reading the rest of the year!

Incidentally, one of those responsible for returning the park to City ownership was George Baer, who in 1878 was a lawyer representing the Philadelphia and Reading Railroad, and who lived only a few blocks from the park, on Eckert Avenue and Mineral Spring Road.

* In 1998, the City of Reading celebrated its "Bicenquinquagenary", or 250th anniversary. True, it had been 250 years since the "town" of Reading was founded in 1748. But, technically, the City of Reading was really only celebrating its Sesquicentennial, or 150th anniversary in 1998, which it had claimed to celebrate in 1898.

It should be remembered that the "City" of Reading only existed as of 1848- before that, it had been a "borough".

This could become a bone of contention for the picky among us in 2048, when the City attempts to celebrate its 300th anniversary, but will really only be celebrating its 200th.

Part 5- The Neversink Mountain Railroad

To better understand the late 19th Century development of Neversink Mountain, we must first consider the development of the railway that would link the various attractions on the mountain.

The Neversink Mountain Railroad Company was actually the second of three companies that were formed in 1889 to develop Neversink Mountain as a picnic and resort area, and to build a mountain railway.

The first was the "Heiner's Spring Company," which had already existed for a few years before the announcement of plans to develop the mountain in late June of 1889. The company, "in connection" with the Philadelphia and Reading Railroad, would "improve and prepare the beautiful Klapperthal valley for a fine pic-nic grove."

The Heiner's Spring Company also proposed to build an electric railroad in the valley. At this point, the plans appeared to only include the Klapperthal area of the mountain. (This appears to be in competition with another scheme. Earlier, in 1888, application had been made for the "St. Lawrence R. R. Company", whose route might have included a wind around the base of Neversink Mountain to Klapperthal.)

The Heiner's Spring Company, an association of George Baer- a lawyer representing the P&R- along with "a number of Reading's foremost citizens and capitalists," included William D. Smith, William McIlvain, Richard T. Leaf, the Kendall Brothers, and George Brooke.

Two weeks later, another company was formed, The Neversink Mountain Railroad Company, consisting of- well, see list above. The purpose was the same as before, but larger, to include the entire mountain.

Then, less than two weeks later, still another company was formed- "The Klapperthal Company"- which would deal strictly in real estate, to buy up tracts of land totaling 850 acres which would be necessary for the construction of the railway. The directors? See list above.

One can almost see the mental wheels turning. The "Heiner's Spring Company," which probably sounded like a good name at the beginning, was abandoned in favor of "The Neversink Mountain Railroad Company." But, since "railroad" was part of the name, George Baer would prudently have decided to distance himself from it, since he was representing the P&R Railroad at the time. So his name is missing from the Neversink Mountain Railroad list of directors. But he's back on the roster for the Klapperthal Company, since it was only a real estate company, and not a conflict.

The Philadelphia and Reading Railroad- which already controlled coal and other cargo between Philadelphia and Reading, including what little was left by then of the Schuylkill Canal business- would be "materially aiding" the project.

So a beautiful pic-nic area (the word was hyphenated in those days) and a scenic mountain railway in the Reading area were seen as an attractive selling tool to get vacationers to come to Reading from Philadelphia and New York. The plans also included a "pavilion" at Klapperthal, which would be the center of activity in the area, and the money-making attraction.

The railway route was not planned at random. The design took into account three existing attractions on the mountain- The White House Hotel/Tavern, The Centennial Springs Hotel, and the Highland House Hotel. None of these enterprises had anything to do with the railroad. So it can only be assumed that their inclusion in the route was a "good neighbor" gesture by the railway. And, oddly enough, all of these attractions outlasted anything that the railway built on the mountain.

Though the typical trip on the Neversink Mountain Railway would begin in Reading, and begin its ascent on the mountain's westernmost end, at the terminus of what used to be the South Ninth Street Trolley, construction of the railway actually began at the eastern end, at Klapperthal, on July 20,

1889. A crew of 75 men began grading the roadway in July, with picks and shovels, and by October, the crew had doubled to 150 men, aided by eleven horses.

The crew did a splendid job, surprisingly quickly (considering the lack of power equipment); and by February of 1890, the grading was complete.

The typical railway bed begins with stone or gravel, which must be brought in from another location. But Neversink Mountain is mostly gravel to begin with- it just needed to be crushed. So, a system of cable buckets was devised, to transport the rough gravel down the south face of the mountain, to a crusher set up near the P&R tracks.

Most of the crushed gravel was then sent back up the mountain, to be used as railway bed. Once grading for the beds had been completed, there was actually an excess of gravel. The excess was used to improve the beds of the P&R Railroad below.

Present-day hikers will notice several concrete structures on the south face, about halfway up the mountain behind the Poplar Neck curve. These concrete stanchions were built as anchors for the cable car gravel operation. They look like they could easily withstand another 100 years on the mountain.

(**Note**: If you are a "Neversink Novice," you may need to refer to the map until you become more familiar with the names and locations). Walking along the south face of Neversink today on one of the railway beds where the concrete stanchions remain, it's difficult to imagine workers being able to negotiate buckets of stone down the face of the mountain. How would they get past all those trees? But in 1890, there were fewer trees along that face of the mountain to interfere with a gravel bucket. This would have made a ride on the Neversink railway in this area kind of like a roller coaster ride, with a steep downhill view of a few hundred feet unobstructed by anything.

One of the concrete stanchions supporting the gravel buckets for the crusher at the base of Neversink Mountain. Photo- Paul A. Druzba

Train or Trolley?

The Neversink Mountain Railroad was designed to use standard-gauge railroad track, 4 ft. 8 ½ inches apart, with 56-pound steel rails. This was different from the trolley track gauge, which was 5 ft. 2 ½ inches. The tie system was railroad standard- 26 inches apart, and the bed of ballast was two feet deep.

Since the trolley line already existed along the railway's first leg, between Penn Street and the White House Tavern at the end of South 9th, adjustment along the trolley line would have to be made to accommodate the mountain railway's standard railroad gauge.

It was decided that the trolley track would stay, and additional track, alongside the trolley track, would be laid for the Neversink line. This was not a popular decision among the people who lived along South 9th Street, who feared that the additional traffic might cause accidents.

Before the new track and wiring could be completed from Reading along South 9th Street, the track-layers went on strike, to improve their wage from $1.25 per day to $1.50 per day. (Look at that last line again- it's $1.50 per DAY, not per hour). The track-layers were promptly fired by the company, and replaced so that the work could continue.

While the ties and rails were being installed on Neversink Mountain, workers were also busily engaged in landscaping. Trees were being removed to improve the view, especially at places like "Point Lookout" near the middle summit. At some of the railway stations, decorative perennial ground covers were planted. They truly were perennial- you can still see them in several places, more than 100 years later!

To the average passenger on the Neversink Mountain Railway, the difference in rail gauge was of no consequence- riders still referred to the railway cars as "trolleys", because they looked like trolleys. Despite some hand-colored postcards to the contrary, the railway cars were actually painted green and cream, the same colors as the Reading trolleys. The cars were built by the J. G. Brill Company of Philadelphia.

Note: An interesting contrast between the 19th Century and the 21st is the cost relationship between labor and materials. In the 1800s, labor was extremely cheap, due to the abundance of inexpensive, yet talented manpower from Europe and the Far East.

Materials were relatively expensive, because the still-developing Industrial Revolution had not yet had a chance to lower the cost of materials substantially by way of mass production. Nails, which had always been prized by early settlers, were just beginning to be produced at a factory in nearby Birdsboro. In the 21st Century, mass production has drastically lowered the cost of materials, but the price of labor has skyrocketed.

The Grand Opening

On July 23, 1890, when the electric railway was just about ready to open to the general public, George Baer, accompanied by officers of the railway, conducted a trial run of the railway from Klapperthal to 9th and Penn Streets- using steam-powered locomotives.

Reality Check: You'll recall that the railway was designed to be "electrified," powered by the same thing that powered the trolleys of Reading. So why is an electrified railway being demonstrated using steam power?
The railway company knew there was a problem with the railway's electric power system, but they needed to open as soon as possible.

On July 31, 1890, the line was officially and hurriedly opened to the public, and the first car of 40 passengers left Ninth and Penn Streets, headed for Klapperthal. The first passengers bought their tickets for the new Neversink Railway at Roland's Cigar Store at Ninth and Penn. The ticket office was later changed to Griesemer's Drug Store. This intersection was a true crossroads in Reading. To the north, the sign read "Kutztown Road." To the south, it read "Philadelphia Road".

(Remember that the Neversink Mountain Railway, like present day tourist attractions and theme parks, had a limited season, so time was of the essence. If the railway was to make any money in 1890 with its open cars, it had to make it before the onset of cold weather).

At the White House Hotel, the passengers on this maiden voyage were transferred to P&R steam coaches, pulled by a borrowed 25-ton steam locomotive from the P&R.

All told, between 500 and 600 passengers rode the Neversink Mountain Railway that first day. Unfortunately for one of the mid-day excursions, the steam locomotive broke a spring and quit at Klapperthal, forcing the passengers to choose between walking back for several miles along the railway bed, or catching a steamboat back to Reading.

But the crisis was seen differently by Mr. Mullholland, the superintendent of the railway, who claimed that the railway had "sufficient facilities to bring them home in good time." Apparently, the passengers were skeptical about what "in good time" meant.

The opening day also suffered another setback when a car jumped the tracks up at the Highland House, but no one was injured in the mishap.

Top: A P&R RR steam engine, used in the early days of the Neversink Mountain Railroad, before the electric power became reliable.
Bottom: An electric car passes two water barrels which were used during the steam power days.
Photos: Meiser- Echoes of Scholla, Passing Scene

Power Shortage

The electric power for the railway was initially provided by a hydroelectric power plant, constructed along the Schuylkill River at Dam #24, commonly known as the "Big Dam", at Lewis' Lock, below Klapperthal Park. Even before the opening day unfolded, the owners knew that the power plant would have trouble supplying enough power under heavy load conditions, and so the railway was often operated by steam power for a few years, until a new power plant could be built and the cars upgraded.

The first power house generated 1,000 horsepower of electric power from Edison electric generators, which were connected to the water turbines at the dam.

This was initially thought to be enough to power four cars at a time on the mountain. The engineers even coordinated a system to minimize power consumption. As two cars were going up the mountain, the other two would be coming down.

But the railway quickly realized that more than four cars would be needed to supply the demand, especially during the tourist season, when as many as twelve cars would be pressed into service.

Two additional cars were ordered from Brill in 1891, and two more were added in 1892 as demand increased.

The river, which supplied hydroelectric power for the railroad, also played a major role in power difficulties. When the river was high and demand was not, power was sufficient. But low river level or increased demand would send the railways scurrying for steam locomotives.

So a new power plant was built in 1894, with four 150-Horsepower coal-fired burners. A coal chute was constructed along the P&R line near the plant, and the coal that was dumped there would be hauled in dump carts to the plant by the operator. Yes, the power plant was a one-man show.

(Part of the plan for the new power plant was to sell power to the Reading trolley system in the winter when the Neversink Railway would not be operated. This proved to be prophetic).

Each car initially featured two 25-horsepower motors, which was later increased in power because of the higher power demands of reaching the triple peaks of Neversink. The Neversink Mountain Railroad was only the third electric-powered railroad in the United States, and the first to be operated by water power. Like many new technologies, it proved to be an exercise in trial and error.

The construction project cost what was then the enormous amount of $250,000, and eventually wound eight miles around Neversink. The crippling cost of construction would eventually seem minor compared to the cost of maintaining this ambitious enterprise.

*Top: The Klapperthal Power House, looking east.
Bottom: The turbine inside the power house. A one-man operation!
Photos: Meiser- Echoes of Scholla*

The Mountain Circuit

A passenger on the Neversink Mountain Railway could simply take the picnic route, riding from Ninth and Penn to the White House Hotel to Klapperthal and back, and many picnickers did just that. This run was known as the "Short Line"- a railroad term you might be familiar with, reprised in a board game which originated in the depression era of the 1930s.

To access the north side of the mountain- the one facing Reading- a switch was employed. Just east of the White House, the car seats were reversed, (since there was no place for the cars to turn around), and the car would take all passengers up Nanny Goat Hill.

About 300 feet up the hill, there was a switch, where the cars could either be directed downhill to the "Short Line" to Klapperthal, or farther uphill for the full circuit. (It should be remembered that railroad "switches" were not electrical contraptions, but manual movement of track by men.)

Passengers taking the full circuit traveled up and around the western peak of Neversink, about halfway up the slope of the hill, and across the north slope of the mountain, with some spectacular views of East Reading.

The car would pass Haak's Cave, then travel over top of the Highland House's Incline Plane Railway by means of a bridge, which needed to be built by the Neversink Railway because the incline plane was there first. The next stop was Hiener's Wissel (Hiener's Spring Park).

At the eastern end of the mountain, at "Observation Point," the view was nothing short of spectacular. On a clear day, a passenger could see Carsonia Park, and all the way to Oley.

Circling the eastern peak of the mountain, there was, almost immediately, another stop on the south side of the peak. This stop was initially used as the station for Graeff's Centennial Springs Hotel, (though not a very convenient one for Graeff's customers). The real purpose of the station was for the Neversink Mountain Hotel, which would soon be built on the eastern peak.

The car then continued west on a rising grade, toward Point Lookout at the summit of the middle peak. Passing back over to the north face, the car continued on its journey along the crest, crossing over again to the north side toward the Highland House, and turned southward for the descent toward Klapperthal.

A third of the way along the south face, the car would pass the Short Line Junction, where cars returning from Klapperthal would veer farther south for the last leg to the White House via a cutoff junction on Nanny Goat Hill. Here, and throughout the route, there were "bypass" sections, where a car could wait while another car passed in the opposing direction.

If you were out for a picnic at Klapperthal Park, you would get off at Klapperthal Park Station, at the eastern end of Klapperthal Glen, after crossing a huge wooden trestle that was built over Klapperthal Glen and the creek far below.

If you were headed for some bowling, baseball or beer down at Klapperthal Pavilion, you'd continue on. The trolley would leave Klapperthal Park Station, circling Klapperthal Park's eastern end, cross the creek again at ground level this time, and head south toward Klapperthal Station.

Looking at the map, the Pavilion seems to be a lot closer to the railway just north of the Pavilion, but it would have been impractical to get off there, because of the steep slope leading down to the Pavilion. So, although it was costly to build a trestle across Klapperthal Glen, it was still cheaper than the alternative.

A trip to the mountain was surprisingly quick and cheap. A passenger leaving the Neversink Mountain trolley stop at 9th and Penn Streets would reach the Observation Point stop at the far end of Neversink Mountain in only 15 minutes, and the round trip, which completely surrounded the mountain, was only 20 cents, later increased to a quarter. This information is available from copies of "The Neversink Item", which were published by the railway company during the line's heyday. In its earlier days, short trips on the railroad could be had for a nickel.

Those who collect old postcards of Reading, including this author, know that the cards showing railway cars on Neversink are some of the most common cards available, for the railway was considered quite an attraction at the end of the 19th Century, which was the beginning of peak postcard use in America.

A familiar scene on Reading, Pa. postcards. This early version, published about 1903, was later reproduced in hand-colored versions, whose hues varied widely. Car colors were not always accurate.
Paul A. Druzba

(Remember that the telephone did not exist at the time, and the only means of quick, short-term communication was the postcard. Mail was delivered three times a day, and a postcard sent in the early morning from one end of Reading would arrive by noon the same day at the other end of town. Not as quick as email, but your investment was just one penny for the card and one penny for the stamp).

The Neversink Mountain Railroad transformed the face of Neversink Mountain. Suddenly, local investors did not need to be persuaded any longer by the P&R RR about the potential for developing Neversink. They saw gold in them thar hills, the same way that 21st Century entrepreneurs see gold at the exits of limited access highways.

(Meiser: Passing Scene)

The Safety Issue

Over on Mount Penn, the Gravity Railroad, which was powered by steam engine up to the peak at the Tower Hotel, and then "let loose" to gravitate its way back down the mountain, suffered the shortcoming of several sharp curves, resulting in a few serious crashes, and more than a dozen deaths over its years of operation.

This lesson was not lost on the builders of the Neversink Mountain Railway. In its 27-year history, the Neversink Mountain Railroad was relatively accident-free compared to its Mount Penn rival.

Neversink smoothed three sharp curves on its line early on, in 1890. After that, passengers beginning their descent from the peaks of the mountain were told by their conductor that none of the curves they would encounter would exceed 30%. But the railway's safety record was not without blemish.

In the early 1900s, a very young girl wandered out onto South 9th Street in the path of an oncoming Neversink Mountain Railroad car, and was killed. The car was traveling about six miles an hour at the time of the accident.

The cars would ascend the mountain at about the same rate, but would gain speed considerably when going downhill.

Freeman Pauley of Klapperthal Road in Exeter was 82 years old in 2002, and remembered stories from his father William, who rode the Neversink Railroad on his way to a picnic at the Klapperthal Pavlion. William Pauley told Freeman of how the Neversink trolleys would whiz down the tracks on a downhill run, so fast that his "coattails would be flying."

Freeman's mother was a Hiester, and so he also remembers hearing about the steamboats which landed on the Schuylkill banks down by Klapperthal Station. As a relation, she would have talked about "Johnny Hiester's steamboats."

Another scary incident occurred in the fall of 1892. A man, "whose bump of indiscretion is abnormally developed" according to the *Berks and Schuylkill Journal*, was among a car-full of passengers headed uphill from the White House. Seeing another car in the distance, the man cried out "Here comes another car!", causing a panic. Several women jumped off the car in terror, thinking there would be a collision, and tumbled over a four-foot retaining wall.

Several broken bones, contusions and bruises were suffered by the women, despite the fact that the "other car" was at least 100 yards away and on another track. The account includes no mention of consequence for the man with poor judgment.

Dollars and Cents

The tremendous cost of the railway's construction was only worsened by its staggering maintenance costs. Consider the upgrades of the electric power system, which included the upgrading of the cars for higher power. The constant track maintenance. The salaries of the drivers, mechanics, station employees and maintenance crews.

The rising costs only got worse as the line, cars and facilities began to age. Despite the fact that as many as 120,000 people a season paid to ride the railway, the revenue never really caught up with costs. The price of a ticket was already a bit higher than a Reading trolley, so increases were not an option.

In 1901, eleven years after the railway's opening, George Baer realized that the railway, and his investments in facilities on Neversink, had been a mistake. (This also happened to be the year in which George Baer became President of the Philadelphia and Reading Railroad, and moved himself and his family to Philadelphia).

The sheriff of Berks County seized all the property of the Neversink Mountain Railroad, including the railway itself, the Klapperthal Pavilion, and the railway's car barns at 9th and Bingaman Streets. On February 16th of that year, the line was sold to pay off its debts.

The buyer was John A. Rigg, president of the United Traction Company (Reading's trolley lines). Rigg had experience in making trolley lines profitable, and had been instrumental in developing Carsonia Park at the far eastern end of Reading's trolley system.

He had also been president of Reading City Council from 1887 to 1890, when the Neversink Mountain Railway was being planned and started. It's not that politics had anything to do with the sale- it's more a matter of "who you know." Rigg would have been in awe of Baer's power, and Baer would have wondered why Rigg could make an electric trolley pay, while he could not.

For a while, the future of the Neversink Mountain Railway seemed to brighten. At its peak, cars left the Railway's 9th and Penn station for Neversink every twenty minutes on Sundays and holidays, from 7 a.m. to midnight. The railway was one of Reading's biggest attractions. But, like most attractions, the novelty eventually wears off.

The Neversink Mountain Railroad was done in by the same thing that had done in the Schuylkill Canal- a more popular form of transportation. By around 1915, the automobile was beginning to leave the horse and buggy, and the Neversink Mountain Railroad, in its dust.

By the summer of 1917, ridership on the railway had declined, while maintenance costs continued to rise. Needed repairs were being left wanting. At the end of that season, rather than continue to throw good money after bad, the new owners decided that 1917 would be the last year for the Neversink Mountain Railway.

The line was abandoned, its cars incorporated into the Reading trolley system. The track was torn up and sold for scrap. Today, proud collectors show off their railroad spikes and plates from the Neversink, which are becoming harder and harder to find.

Note: Although the track was removed long ago, there is still one rail from the Neversink Mountain Railway, mysteriously buried "on end", sticking straight up out of the ground. The rail appears in the Klapperthal area, which admittedly is a large area to search.

(Foesig: Trolleys of Berks County)

Other Railway Notes

A Third Power Plant?

According to many published sources, the "updated" power plant, built in 1894, was the one which was destroyed by the flood of 1942. But there seems to have been a third.

According to the Reading Eagle in 1917, the "updated" power plant at Klapperthal was destroyed by a fire in 1913, when the Neversink Mountain Railway was owned by the Reading trolley system.

Due to declining ridership, a new power plant probably would not have been in the budget for the Reading trolley system. So power for the Neversink railway would have been taken from the City's trolley system for the remainder of the mountain railway's life.

In 1917, the Metropolitan Power Company, later Met Ed, which had owned the plant, decided to re-build it, at a cost of $100,000.

Even though the Neversink Mountain Railway would no longer exist after that time, hydroelectric power was considered by Metropolitan to be much more cost-effective than coal. So it was worth the investment.

The Metropolitan power plant at the Big Dam ran smoothly for the next 25 years, until it was destroyed by a flood which also wiped out the Big Dam. At the time, the original portion of the dam was revealed, including a brownstone with the date "1820" carved on it, showing the date of the dam's construction.

Remnants of this, the third power plant at the site, can still be seen by taking a walk down Klapperthal Creek, under a tunnel beneath the old P&R RR tracks, and turning left. Part of the remnants include walled troughs, into which coal was dumped to power the turbines, and the remnants of maintenance sheds where the cars were repaired.

Some brick remnants of the original power plant can also be seen slightly to the west of the concrete foundations of the later plants.

The tunnel, which was built in 1926, (you can see the date in the concrete, inside a Reading Railroad logo), was designed to be an access to the power plant by automobile, for maintenance purposes. The tunnel was also designed to carry the water from Klapperthal Creek, <u>underneath</u> the road surface, to the river.

This underground water passage was prone to clogging, and eventually the water from the creek flowed OVER the road surface. This resulted in severe erosion on the Schuylkill River side of the tunnel, which has been nicely repaired by volunteers of the Schuylkill River Greenway Association. The water is now collected on the river side of the tunnel by new construction of the Exeter Bike Trail.

Before and After: Top- the final Klapperthal power plant at the Big Dam, around 1930. Bottom- The dam broke in the flood of 1942, revealing a stone with "1820" carved in it- a remnant of the canal building days. (Meiser)

Klapperthal Creek, one of the few open water sources on Neversink, was actually not named until the 20th Century, and the LATE 20th Century at that. Robert Bartmann, a geologist who does volunteer work for the Berks County Conservancy, claims to have named the creek in a drawing of the area a number of years ago, and the name followed onto more contemporary drawings. In the hustle-bustle growth spurt of the late 19th Century, no one thought of actually naming the creek.

"The cars," as described by Exeter Township historian Earl Ruppert, "were open, some with seats the width of the car, others with an aisle in the middle. In case of rain, the motorman had to stand out in it (the rain)." The cars had no air brakes, only hand brakes. Yet their safety record was superior to the gravity system employed over on Mount Penn.

The Railroad's standard stable of eight cars were numbered one through eight, and were all built by J. G. Brill, although some people claim that car #8 was actually a Pullman. The cars were all eventually re-fitted in the Reading Traction Company shops, re-numbered, and put into service in the Reading trolley system.

In 2002, there is a wooden bridge which covers what remains of the original pond at Klapperthal Park. If you're standing on the bridge and look left, you'll see stone walls built along the creek's banks. At this point, trolleys circling Klapperthal Park paused, and were inspected by men below, from underneath the car.

It sounds like a sloppy job but, in the days of the railway, the creek actually flowed several feet to the west of where it does now, so the inspectors were not standing in the creek while they worked.

The Changing Scenery

Postcards of the day show spectacular scenes from both faces of the mountain. The most common view was one from Point Lookout, which looked down, unobstructed, on the horseshoe curve in the Schuylkill River from the mountain's south face. The scene is still pretty spectacular today, but has been largely obscured by the growth of trees.

From the Highland House, one could once see a mostly unobstructed view of east Reading, and the view from the highest, easternmost peak is also now mostly obscured.

These old views, though spectacular, were made possible only by human intervention- first, by the railroad, clearing beds for the tracks and landscaping for maximum viewing beauty, and then by loggers stripping the mountain faces of trees.

The loggers couldn't have cared less about a view- they were only trying to collect lumber for building homes, or heating ones already built.

But the railroad was very interested in views, to please the riders of the railway.

The views from Neversink today are, except for a commercial venture and some homes, mainly as they would have appeared to the Lenni Lenape, before 1700, and the coming of the Europeans.

The view from Point Lookout, as it appeared about 1905. The view was made possible by extensive clearing, evidenced by the cleared timber visible at lower right. (Paul Druzba)

Top: Tiller (brakeman) was the great-great-grandfather of Gloria Meiser, wife of George. Bottom: Car #4 crosses the wooden trestle at Klapperthal. (Meiser)

Top: Cigar ad from 1893. (Representative Business Men of Reading).

Bottom: Car #2 awaits a "switch". The switcher is crouched by the pole. (George M. Meiser IX)

Part 6- The Resorts

Eventually, all of the hotels on Neversink would come to be known as "resorts," although the owners of some would probably have chaffed at the term. The word "resort" was a railroad concoction, to give the impression to jaded out-of-towners that these were above-average accommodations. And some truly were. But at least one of the "resorts" didn't offer accommodations at all.

Since two of the enterprises on Neversink Mountain- The White House Hotel/Tavern and The Highland House Hotel- both pre-dated the Neversink Mountain Railroad, it's only right that they should be mentioned first.

Reminder- "The Resorts" section is divided into "Chapters," each one covering a resort facility, with its accompanying stop number on the railway. There won't be a "Stop #1" listing, because Stop #1 was Ninth and Penn, where riders from Reading boarded the Neversink Mountain Railway for a trip to the mountain.

Note- The "stops" on the railway should not be taken literally. Although they all existed at one time or another during the 27 years of the railroad's existence, not all ever appeared on a ticket at one time. Some stops appeared later, and some disappeared after a few years. They do, however, represent the route that the railway took on a circuit around Neversink Mountain.

Chapter 1- The White House (Stop #2)

In 1753, just a few years after Thomas and Richard Penn laid out the street plan for the new town of Reading, a new road opened between Reading and Flying Hills. This new road crossed the western end of Neversink, and was a continuation of South 9th Street, which had originally ended around the site of the former Reading Brewery.

At first, the new road was called "Neversink Road," but was later changed to the Whitehouse Road, as a result of the earliest commercial venture on the mountain, the White House Tavern (Hotel).

(Residents of Exeter Township know that there is now another "Neversink Road," running from the 422 Bypass at the Mount Penn exit, south toward the river, west along the railroad tracks, and north toward Mount Penn, passing Forest Hills cemetery at Klapperthal, at the back of which is one of the more popular hiking entrances to Neversink).

The Whitehouse Road intersected the site of a later road, which is now known as Route 422- the West Shore Bypass. (This is one of those names that many people don't even think about- "West Shore" refers to the west shore of the Schuylkill River, which the bypass follows).

Retired General George M. Keim, who had seen some action in the War of 1812, acquired the land surrounding the site of his future venture around 1832, and built the White House tavern about 1840, near the crest of the slope of Neversink at the easternmost reaches of the City of Reading. It was strategically placed at just the spot where horses (and people) would need to be watered after the long climb up the hill from the Schuylkill River.

The hotel was located on the western (river) side of White House Road. Another factor in its location is Neversink Spring, which also made it the ideal location for a bottling works, built across the road from the Tavern/hotel.

With the abundance of breweries in Reading at the time, and the abundance of wineries on Neversink and Mount Penn, it's impossible to imagine nothing but spring water being served at the tavern, and weary travelers were no doubt looking for something foamy or fruity to quench their thirst.

The hotel was a two-story structure with attic, built overlooking the precipice over the Philadelphia and Reading railroad tracks. (And a precipice it is- the slope down to the river at this point is quite steep).

The hotel had three side porches, overlooking the river and tracks below. The view included bridges over the Schuylkill which had been built to accommodate the P&R Railroad.

From the east veranda of the hotel, one could see the huge slag bank, created by Eckert's Henry Clay furnace. The west veranda offered a view of the Reading Iron Works (see postcard picture).

Across the Whitehouse Road from the hotel was the White House bottling works, which took advantage of the spring.

The hotel went through a succession of owners over the years after Mr. Keim's passing in 1861. John L. Lawrence took over ownership of the hotel in 1894, soon after the creation of the mountain railway. After his death in 1905, he was succeeded by his son, Richard L., who had operated successful hotels at 12th and Cotton, and 10th and Muhlenberg.

The downfall of the hotel began in 1920, with the arrival of Prohibition. While other, more remote hotels on Neversink would prosper as speakeasies during the next 12 years, the White House was too close to Reading and its police to survive that way.

Today, only a foundation remains of the bottling works, and is best seen in very early spring, before leafing has occurred. Walk on Whitehouse Road a few hundred yards beyond the corner of 9th and South. There's no need to be more specific about location here. If you pass the foundations and can't see them, you need to see an optometrist.

You'll see the foundations of the White House Bottling Works on the left. To the right is an overgrowth of shrubs and weeds, the former site of the Tavern/hotel. Bottles from the White House Bottling Works can still be had occasionally on Internet auctions. I gave up on one of these auctions when the bidding reached 30 dollars.

Standing on the back porch of the White House, this was the view of the southwestern portion of Reading, including the Reading Iron Works. (Paul Druzba)

Top: Rare view from the south side of the White House, showing people waiting for a trolley. Bottom: Trolley stop #2, The White House Hotel on the right, with the bottling works on the left (Meiser: Echoes of Scholla, Passing Scene)

Interesting facts about the area-

1. Just beyond the Tavern on the Whitehouse Road was a promontory referred to as "Lover's Leap." According to "legend," a native American couple leapt to their deaths from this point, which was removed in railroad construction around the turn of the 20th Century. Were there really lovers who leapt from Lover's Leap? Probably not. No one on record had ever heard of "Lover's Leap" until it appeared in promotional literature for The Neversink Mountain Railroad. Lover's Leap is probably nothing more than an advertising copywriter's daydream.

2. Family burial plots were still fairly common in the late 19th Century, and there is written record of the grandparents and great-grandparents of Isaac W. Levan, founder of the former Penn National Bank at 8th and Penn Streets, being buried just above the site of the White House Tavern. This family was known for being a bit "peculiar," and one of them is said to have been buried in an iron coffin which was open at both ends, in case he needed to "escape."

3. Another unique feature of the area is a cave, located on the Whitehouse Road, which served as an underground storage facility for the Deppen Brewery, and is the only part of the city which is owned by the City on the surface (10th and South Playground), and by

private interests below the surface! The beer cave was dug sometime around 1850.

4. There is also written record that a sign reading "Fisherman's Retreat" once adorned the White House Tavern. Speculation has been made that the Tavern was a retreat for fisherman enjoying the bounty of catfish and sunfish from one of the best fishing holes in Reading, in the Schuylkill, down Whitehouse Road. They certainly would have NEEDED a retreat after climbing back up the hill past the hotel towards Reading!

5. "Nanny Goat Hill" was a name that was given to the area above the 10th and South Playground, and uphill from the White House Tavern- because goats raised by the immigrants who lived in the neighborhood, "Irishtown," used to graze on the hill. A video, "Reading, Willing and Able," produced by VideoWorks Production Company in Reading from a black and white film shot in 1948 during the city's Bicentennial, shows a float from 10th and South Playground, and a banner which reads, "Once Nanny Goat Hill, now Tenth and South." In the early days of the railway, its owner heard complaints from the drivers about the nanny goats on Nanny Goat Hill, especially about one bock (male goat) which was especially troublesome and liked to stand on the tracks when a car was coming. The drivers were afraid the bock would be hit. The owner countered by offering a prize of ten dollars to the crew of the car that DID hit

the bock. There is no record of a payoff. Speaking of nanny goats, it turns out that this was not the only "Goat Hill" on Neversink. (More later).

6. General Keim, the builder of the hotel, was well-connected nationally. The Historical Society of Berks County has hand-written lyrics to the National Anthem, sent to General Keim by Francis Scott Key. Locally, Keim was one of the founding members of the Berks County Agricultural and Horticultural Society. He was the Society's president in 1854 when the county commissioners leased 39 of the 50 acres of Penn's Common (City Park) to the Society for one dollar a year, for the purpose of an annual exhibition (county fair). In 1887, this lease was declared illegal by the Pennsylvania courts, and the grounds were returned to the citizens of Reading.

7. Down the hill and to the northwest, near the bank of the Schuylkill, once stood "Keim's Folly." General Keim had a large mound of earth constructed, in steps, which were to be turned into some sort of "Gardens of Babylon." The formative stages of this venture, which was never completed, can be seen in a painting at the Historical Society of Berks County.

8. The White House Hotel was the first commercial hotel on Neversink. Which one was the last? The answer at the end of the book.

Top: 19th Century painting that shows "Keim's Folly", the layered structure in middle right. (Historical Society of Berks County)
Bottom: The door that bars the beer cave under 10th & South Playground, early spring. (Photo: Paul Druzba)

Chapter 2-
The Highland House
(Stop #7)

The White House Hotel may have started as a hotel, with paying staying guests. In its later years, however, it was reduced to a "watering hole", and eventually as a residence for the proprietors of the bottling works. (More on that later). But as early as 1883, two people saw the possibilities of establishing and running a proper hotel on Neversink.

Joseph Ganser of Reading had hotel experience. In 1866, he had become the proprietor of the Keystone House (later called the Hotel Penn) on the northwest corner of 6th and Penn Streets in Reading.

In the early 1880s, Ganser and his daughter Alice, a Reading schoolteacher, acquired 80 acres on the western peak of Neversink Mountain. From that vantage point 728 feet above the Schuylkill River, they could no doubt see the steady stream of P&R RR trains, freight as well as passenger, passing in both directions just below their mountain acquisition. There was money to be made from all those visitors, as well as from the citizens of the increasingly-overcrowded City of Reading.

The Highland House was 115 feet wide across the front, offered 118 rooms, and was built mostly of wood.

In an 1893 ad in the "Neversink Item," published "in behalf of Amusement and Reading's Business Interests" by H.W. Brooks, the Highland House was billed as a "health and pleasure resort," where one could "board by the day, week or month," and where meals and refreshments were "made to order, and served on short notice."

An advertising brochure for the Highland House stated that it was furnished with the best furniture throughout, "far superior to the kind generally put in hotels." It also offered electric lights and bells (a novelty in that era), and steam heat.

It was referred to as "The Switzerland of America," a moniker later adopted by the town of Jim Thorpe, Pa., formerly Mauch Chunk. (God bless Jim Thorpe the man, but I hereby cast my vote for a return to Mauch Chunk, PA. They can keep "The Switzerland of America" though).

Rates were listed as "between 8 and 15 dollars per week," and "transient" guests were charged between 2 and 2 ½ dollars per day. Guests also received discount tickets for the Neversink Mountain Railway.

The Highland House was the scene of various conventions, and proved to be a very popular resort- at first for locals, but later mostly for out-of-towners, and finally, at its end, for locals again. A "Reading Weekly Eagle" item later stated that "this place has been filled each

A page from the Neversink Item, with an ad for the Highland House, a "Health and Pleasure Resort." (Meiser- Passing Scene)

season since it was erected. The guests are mostly from Philadelphia, New York and surrounding cities. Mrs. Alice Ganser Light is the proprietor. She says that the tendency of late years is to make short trips to the seashore, and then to the mountains."

Although the Highland House was originally intended only as a hotel, offering lodging and meals to its guests, that role expanded with the coming of the Neversink Mountain Railway. In the early 1890s, a beer garden and dance pavilion were built by the Railroad on land they owned adjacent to the Highland House property, to take advantage of the short-term visitors who passed by The Highland House in great numbers on weekends. The Gansers even had a roller coaster there for one year.

(Meiser)

The Incline Plane Railway

Incline plane railways (basically diagonal elevators) became very popular in the 1880s, and the most famous and well known were built in Pittsburgh and Chattanooga.

In 1883, the Gansers began construction of an incline railway, to bring construction materials up Neversink Mountain to their hotel site, and hopefully to bring up customers after it was built.

Initially, the Incline ran from 13th and South Streets up to the western peak of Neversink, a distance of about a third of a mile. It made use of two sets of railway track and two cars, one ascending while the other descended.

The cars were built high on the back and short on the front, so they and their passengers would sit level on the ride up or down. Just imagine what a car like this would have been like on level track- like being on a thrill ride at Hersheypark!

The cars were connected by heavy steel cable to the engine house, which sat next to the Highland House. The engine house was originally built with a 50-horsepower steam engine to provide the power for the Incline Plane, but the engine was later replaced by an electric motor.

The Incline Plane. Note the NMRR bridge about halfway up, providing shelter for the Incline Plane cars when not in use. S 13th Street today (Meiser- Passing Scene)

(**NOTE**: Back in 1881, two years before the Gansers started work on their incline plane and hotel, another incline plane and resort hotel had been proposed over on Mount Penn. The railway would have run from City Park up to the site of Drenkel's Field, which is now used by hobbyists to fly model airplanes.

The Mt. Penn incline plane and hotel would have cost from $75,000 to $100,000 to build. But the plan was scrapped when Henry and George Eckert, who owned the land where the hotel was proposed, refused to sell. One can almost hear the Gansers saying, "If they won't do it, we will!")

By late 1883, the Gansers' Incline was in operation, and construction of the hotel, to be called The Highland House, was completed in late 1884.

Joseph Ganser, who had been President of Reading City Council from 1879 to 1880, could be described as "feisty". In 1889, the City began legal proceedings to have the incline railway removed. It was claimed to be a "noisy nuisance" at all hours of the day and night.

Also, it ate up a substantial portion of South 13th Street, and the City felt it was preventing the east side of the street from being developed.

Ganser adopted the position, "I was here before the street was." Earlier that year, and no doubt knowing about the plans to build the Neversink Mountain Railroad, Ganser had awarded contracts to build "The Cannonball"- a "mountain railway" toboggan ride on the Highland House grounds on Neversink, with wood planks instead of iron rails. It amounted to nothing more than an amusement ride, and was short lived.

So was Ganser. He did not survive to hear the end of the argument on the incline plane, and died in December, 1889. The argument resulted in a compromise.

Fairview Street, which was a few hundred feet below the bridge where the Neversink Mountain Railroad crossed over the incline, became the end of the Incline's line in 1889. The track between Fairview and South was removed, along with the two story structure that had stood at the bottom of the line at South Street.

Ironically, Ganser's incline railway brought his mourners up to the Highland House, and brought his body back down.

Although it may seem that Ganser intended to compete with the Neversink Mountain Railway with his toboggan, it should be remembered that the original plan for the Neversink Mountain Railway was limited to the south side of the mountain. The toboggan was no doubt intended to provide amusement where the railway did not, from an incline plane railway that traveled where the Neversink railroad did not yet venture. Unfortunately, Ganser did not live to see the Neversink Mountain Railway dropping passengers off at his door. It is unknown whether he even got to see the bridge constructed over his incline plane. Ganser's incline plane railway would benefit from that bridge, which turned out to be an ideal place to park his railway cars when they were not in use, thereby protecting them from the elements.

A 1903 City insurance map of the Highland House property shows the bridge as the "Car House" where the cars were stored. He probably would have chuckled to know that the Neversink Railway had paid to keep his cars out of the weather.

Ganser's feistiness apparently was passed on to his son, A. B. Ganser, who sued a business in east Reading for building a contrivance similar to his father's toboggan roller coaster on Neversink. The suit was unsuccessful.

The Gansers' incline railway ceased operation in 1907, because the Neversink Mountain Railway brought more visitors to the mountain from a more convenient location, in center city. Once the railway began running, ridership on the incline railway dropped dramatically.

Ten years later, when the Neversink Mountain Railway ceased operation and there was no easy way up to the hotel, the Highland House became isolated from the large crowds which had once frequented the mountain resorts, and who now took their business elsewhere. The Highland House went into rapid decline.

As one looked up Neversink Mountain from South 13th Street along the incline railway tracks, The Highland House stood to the left at the top, while the beer garden, roller coaster and dance pavilion were on the right, to the west.

By the time Prohibition was enacted in 1920, the Highland House was already "officially" closed, and the dance pavilion had earlier been dismantled, sold, and apparently moved to Dengler's Glen Hotel over in Klapperthal Glen by means of the Neversink Railway.

Access to the Glen Hotel had remained fairly easy from Exeter Township, and its business had not suffered as much as its higher-elevation neighbor.

Still accessible from some tricky access roads from east Reading, the Highland House served as a speakeasy during the days of Prohibition in the 1920s. Though the hotel was officially listed by the City as "unoccupied" as of 1909, it's lights could still be seen burning in the evenings, catering to thirsty locals.

The Highland House changed hands several times over its life, finally struggling to survive on the clandestine alcohol trade. The owner for the last twenty years was the Barbey family. (I wonder what brand of beer was being served there at the time?) Though the Barbey family did operate a speakeasy on the site during Prohibition, it should also be noted that they owned the Highland House for about ten years before Prohibition began. So the hotel's role as a speakeasy was not their original intent. It was a matter of adapting to changing times.

Still, while Prohibition was in force, the "powers that be" seemed to look the other way regarding the nocturnal activities at the Highland House. When the hotel's demise finally came, the Reading Eagle reported that the Highland House had been unoccupied "for the last fifteen years, it is understood." And as far as the City was concerned, the Barbeys had never occupied the building at all.

Winter view of the Highland House in its last years. Many windows are boarded up. (Meiser- Passing Scene)

The Big Fire

The Barbeys employed a watchman at the hotel in its final years- an elderly man named Lester Fix- and he lived in a small building apart from the hotel, described as a "shanty," and adjacent to a large wooden water tank, which collected precious mountaintop water as it ran off the roof of the hotel in a rain.

Boarded up and looking abandoned, the hotel finally burned to the ground in a spectacular fire on the night of October 25, 1930.

The fire was discovered about 11:30 p.m., and people living at the foot of the mountain said they heard "three large explosions" just before the fire started.

Firefighters from the Union Fire Company responded to alarms, but found the access road to the Highland House so rough that they gave up. By 2 a.m. Sunday, the Highland House had burned to the ground, and nothing was left but smoldering timbers.

The fire could be seen for many miles around. Automobiles in every section of the city were quickly pointed toward Neversink Mountain, and additional police had to be summoned to control a traffic jam on Fairview Street, which was clogged with cars trying to get to the scene of the blaze. (Remember this paragraph when you get to the chapter on the Neversink Mountain Hotel).

By the time the building became an inferno, about 50 people were at the scene, helpless to stop the blaze. Some remembered Mr. Fix wandering about the site with a lantern, looking confused, and not remembering any explosions before the fire began. It seems that Mr. Fix was a VERY sound sleeper.

Fire officials stated that the blaze may have been caused by "incendiarism" (arson- another word which will re-appear in later chapters).

Notes: As a boy in early 20th Century Reading, Laurence Gieringer would gaze out his bedroom window at the twinkling lights of the Highland House high atop Neversink Mountain. Later in life, he decided to recreate that vision of his youth, in a miniature village that mirrored what he saw as a boy. Gieringer's childhood memories became "Roadside America" in Shartlesville- still one of Berks County's most popular and enduring tourist attractions.

Some vintage readers may remember motorcycle races being held on Neversink beginning around the time of the destruction of the Highland House. The races were run on the bed of the old Incline Railway, which was still relatively clear at the time, and was kept that way for at least a generation by the races.

The motorcycle races resulted in ribbons for the winners, but also caused serious erosion on the mountain, and attempts are being made to control this by-product of well-intentioned fun.

Before the arrival of the Neversink Mountain Railway, another incline plane on Neversink had been proposed, from the Woodvale Inn on 23rd Street, up over the mountain to the Centennial Springs Hotel, and down the south face to Dengler's Glen Hotel. It apparently was never more than an idea.

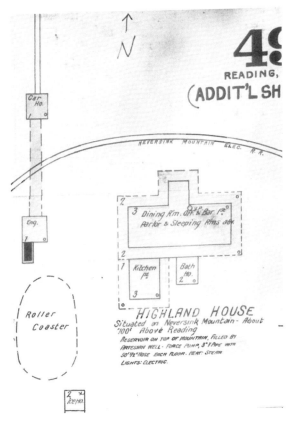

Sketch of the Highland House property from a fire insurance map @1890. Note the Roller Coaster outline, and the protruding bath house in the back, which can be seen on the preceding "winter scene".
(Meiser- Passing Scene)

Top: *Rare view of Highland House from the side. From an early souvenir booklet.*
(Paul Druzba)
Bottom: *The operator of the Incline Plane in the only known picture of the inside of the machine house.*
(Meiser- Passing Scene)

(Top and Bottom: Fun and games at the Highland House in its heyday. (Meiser)

Chapter #3- Haak
(Stop #3)

"Haak" is listed as a "stop" along the Neversink Mountain Railway on a ticket from its early days, but why the railway would stop there is unclear. Perhaps it was a brief stop, to allow passengers to take in the spectacular view of East Reading from above. But more than likely, it was a practical matter.

"Haak's Farm" originated as a 174-acre tract of land, which was sold in the 1770s by its original owner, a Philadelphia lawyer named Richard Peters, to an Episcopal rector from Reading, the Rev. Alexander A. Murray, for 475 pounds.

After the Reverend returned to England in 1778, the land was sold to Michael Krause, who left the land, upon his death in 1804, to his granddaughter Elizabeth, the wife of John Haak. Thereafter, the land became known as "Johnny Haak's Farm."

(Remember that it was only fairly recently that women were allowed to own land in their own name in Pennsylvania. True, many of the names which appear on maps of the area in the 1890s are of women. That's because, when a man died, his wife gained ownership of the land until she remarried).

Eventually, the large tract was split up, and part of it became well-known as a good source of ochre (ocher) on Neversink.

Ochre is a sought-after mineral which was commonly used as a pigment in paint manufacturing in the late 19th Century. Soft and easily pulverized, ochre sports a yellow, brown or red color, depending on the type of ochre and where it is found.

Sometime around 1903, two men were digging sand pits in the area, and came upon a powdery yellowish-brown material. At first, they had no idea what it was. Once they found out it was high-grade sienna, which is a more valuable form of ochre, they realized that they had stumbled onto a sort of gold mine.

The area's mineral rights were soon sold to an Easton, Pa. Company, which began tunneling into the north slope of Neversink. (One of the people connected with that company was a man named Mr. Williams, who would later become famous as the second half of Sherwin-Williams paints.)

The cave/shaft extended about 800 feet into the hillside of Neversink, and before long was producing upwards of 200 tons of sienna per year, valued at the time at about 20 dollars per ton.

Later, when chemical pigments were found that could be substituted for ochre and sienna, the mine was abandoned. But in its heyday, from about 1905 to 1910, Neversink sienna was being shipped in large quantities to another Scranton, Pa. Company- Binney and Smith. For a while, every package of Crayola crayons that left the Scranton plant had a little trace of Neversink Mountain in the box. Remember the color "burnt sienna"? There was a color called "ochre" before that.

Stan Walters, who was 100 years old when I talked to him in 2002, remembered exploring the ochre mine caves as a teenager around the end of World War I. "It was scary. You could get lost in there, and nobody would find you."

Eventually, the ochre/sienna tunnel was blasted shut by the City of Reading for safety reasons. It is said that the local artist, Christopher Shearer, got his ochre from Neversink.

Today, ochre is still used as a pigment, mainly in the construction industry. It is renowned for its longevity, being less susceptible to fading than other chemical pigments.

The "earthtones" of ochre are mixed with concrete for ornamental purposes, and ochre is still used in some paint manufacture. It is still considered one of the finest materials for reproducing "skin" color of every shade.

Haak, or "Hawk" to locals who had never seen it spelled, was situated between the Highland House and Hiener's Wissel on the north face of Neversink, roughly at the location of the area commonly known as the "sand quarry".

That name came from an early 20th Century stone crushing operation on the site, producing gravel and sand for the construction trade, until a fire destroyed the crusher about 1930. The foundation of the crusher can still be seen there.

The stop could have been listed on the railway tickets because of workers who might have labored at the ochre mine at the time. But, considering the fact that it cost at least a dime to take the railway to Haak on a one-way ticket, and many footpaths were available to the site from east Reading, it's doubtful that a low-paid worker would have spent the dime to get to work when he could walk.

Walters, whose father struggled to raise him without his mother in Reading, was in his teens when the trolleys traversed the mountain, but never rode the Neversink Mountain Railway. "I didn't have a dime," he said.

The Haak Cave (Meiser: Echoes of Scholla)

1890s view of Neversink, showing the Highland House roller coaster. Middle right also shows Hiener's Wissel, with some picnickers. Note the sparse East Reading development.
(Meiser- Passing Scene)

Chapter 4
Hiener's Wissel
(stop #4)

Traveling eastward, along the north (Reading) side of Neversink, past Haak's Cave, a rider would next encounter the stop for Hiener's Wissel, probably the most mis-spelled, mis-pronounced, and misunderstood attraction on Neversink Mountain. Let's start with the spelling.

Kraft Hiener was a native of Stuttgart, Germany, and one of the earliest owners of land on Neversink Mountain, although he never lived there. Hiener purchased 30 acres on the north face from Jacob Gugher in 1776, for 10 pounds. (The Declaration of Independence did not include the establishment of the "dollar"- that was still a few years in the future).

The land contained a prolific spring of pure mountain water, and a beautiful meadow. The German word for "meadow" is "wiese," and "a little meadow" in Pennsylvania German is "wiessli."

According to Wayne E. Homan, a late area history buff and Reading Eagle columnist, early residents who did not speak German would write the word as "wissel," and pronounce it as "whistle." So Kraft Hiener's little meadow, "Hiener's Wiessli," became "Hiener's Wissel," or in English, "Hiener's Whistle."

References in news accounts and historical works are about evenly split between "Hiener" and "Heiner". Pronunciation is crucial here, and considering that the pronunciation passed down over the generations is "heener" and not "high-ner," the Hiener spelling is more likely correct. It was listed as "Heiner" early in the Mountain Railway chapter, because that's the way it was spelled in the charter of the company.

Although he never lived on his Neversink property, Mr. Hiener did use stone from the mountain which, according to legend, he and his wife "carried" to the corner of Sixth and Penn Streets in Reading, to build a house there, on the southeast corner.

One can just imagine the muscles bulging on both Hiener and his wife during construction, considering the thousands of trips of several miles each with an unbelievable burden. I'm inclined to think that another interpretation of "carried" is called for. In the 19th Century, "carrying" could also mean employing the use of a horse and wagon. Though Hiener was described as a "burly" man, he was also known for being boastful.

Note: The Hiener house in Reading was subsequently used as a business for many years by the Heitzmann family, and eventually became part of a newer building- Dives, Pomeroy and Stewart- later Pomeroy's.

In 1788, Kraft Hiener sold his farm to his son for 30 pounds. Yes, he actually sold the land to his son, and made a profit of 20 pounds! His son died 20 years later, and the land passed through several hands, including the sheriff's. Other buyers included a group of investors in the Neversink Mountain Railroad, who bought the land for $10,000, and soon after sold it to the railroad for $49,500. Today, they call that "insider trading."

War at the Whistle

In the early summer of 1863, as the Confederate Army was marching into Pennsylvania, the residents of Reading became concerned. VERY concerned. The local militia was recruited and encamped at the head of Penn Street in the common (City Park), but their ranks soon outgrew the site.

The militia was moved to the more spacious meadows at Hiener's Wissel on Neversink Mountain, where there was plenty of good drinking water. And just across Rose Valley (between Neversink and Mount Penn along 19th Street), they could wash their clothes in Rose Valley Creek, which still flows along a site now occupied by a picnic area in Pendora Park.

The militia camp at Hiener's Wissel was named "Camp Peter Muhlenberg," after the revered Revolutionary War general.

In the early days of the Neversink Mountain Railroad, Hiener's Wissel was a popular stop for those packing a picnic lunch. In the railway's later years, the Wissel was used by local religious groups as a site for camp meetings.

In the 1930s, a wall was built around Hiener's Wissel Spring as a community project, with an eagle mounted on the wall. Vandals promptly stuffed rags into the spring's pipe and stole the eagle. (You see? Vandalism did **NOT** begin with **your** generation). The water later flowed from a metal "Lion's Mouth", which also disappeared. The spring is located above Fairview Street, between 18 ½ Street and 19th.

Hiener's Wissel Spring flows down to the low point of the valley, underneath Perkiomen Avenue, where it is joined by water from Rose Valley Creek, on its way to the Schuylkill River.

1969 photo of children playing in the trickle of Hiener's Wissel Spring.
(Reading Eagle Company)

Chapter 5- Neversink Mountain Hotel (Stop #5)

This is one of the shortest- in terms of years- and yet the most interesting story of the resort years on Neversink Mountain.

In the early days of the Neversink Mountain Railroad, cars stopped at a spot called "Observation Point", at the eastern peak and highest location on Neversink. From here, it was often possible to see clear over to the Oley Valley. It was one of the most amazing vistas in Berks.

In the railway's first years, if you turned around and looked behind you from that point, you would see nothing but trees. But the vista behind Observation point was about to turn the focus of the observation inward, toward Neversink Mountain.

By 1890, the Philadelphia and Reading Railroad, as the largest corporation in the world, took pride in providing the very best for its customers, which were increasingly passenger in nature along the railway's original Philadelphia-to-Reading route.

A number of local businessmen and community leaders, including John Barbey (beer), John D. Mishler (retail-dry goods), George Brooke (iron), Morton C. McIlvain (banking and iron), Thomas P. Merritt (lumber, and who was Mayor of Reading at the time), and Moses K. Graeff (who was already the owner of a nearby hotel), were persuaded to invest in a spectacular new hotel, to be built at the highest peak of Neversink Mountain.

This hotel, which was modeled after a big summer hostelry on Manhattan Beach, Long Island, would cater to the out-of-town visitors from Philadelphia and New York, who were accustomed to "better" facilities. The investors were told that the facility would cost $100,000 to build, and they enthusiastically put up a good portion of the money for the project.

In November, 1891, a building contract was issued to Levi H. Focht, who would later build the present Penn Street Viaduct (bridge).

Construction of the massive hotel project was overseen by the officers of the company. Thomas Merritt, who was President of the company, and mayor of Reading, was also the owner of Merritt Lumber.

In those days, liquor licenses were issued by the City, and not by the State, and an applicant was expected to appear at the license hearing. Oddly, the hotel would have no trouble obtaining a liquor license from the City of Reading, despite the fact that its representative did not even show up at the license hearing. It helps to be mayor. But it does NOT help to be a CANDIDATE for mayor, as Mr. Whitman, the builder of the Pagoda, would find out the hard way 15 years later).

The handler of the work horses was a man named Albert W. Kline. He loved to work with horses so much, that he eventually opened a bar (thankfully not called a hotel) named "Al Kline's Paddock" on the southeast corner of Tenth and Franklin Streets in Reading. In it, patrons could actually sit in a saddle while they sipped. Sadly, this unique Reading landmark is now gone.

Al Kline's Paddock as it appeared on a 1950s postcard. Proprietor- Fred Carlance. The phone number was 3-9430
(Paul Druzba)

Locals Not Welcome

From the outset, the Neversink Mountain Hotel was billed as a "visitor's" hotel, and was not promoted or publicized locally at all. Instead, promotional materials, including brochures, were distributed where the patrons were expected to originate- Philadelphia and New York.

These promotional materials continue to be a rare collector's item in the Reading area, since none were distributed here, and out-of-town recipients would have looked on them as "junk mail," and disposed of them exactly the same way that you dispose of yours.

Though the lot surrounding the hotel site was relatively small, only 15 acres, the most would be made of every acre. The grounds included plans for tennis and croquet, "an outdoor pool", and an 800-foot long promenade surrounding the grounds, where guests could stroll, enjoying clean mountain air.

The hotel itself was envisioned on a grand scale, with the intention of satisfying the visitors' wishes for the very finest. The building was 360 feet long, 45 feet wide, and five stories high (including the basement). Since the hotel was built at the peak of the mountain, the advertising brochures insisted that there were no "back rooms." The facility included extra-wide stairs, parlors, reception rooms, a billiard hall, shuffleboard alleys, and dining halls with old-fashioned fireplaces.

The hotel maintained a stable of four horses, which were used by guests for riding, and also to pick up visitors from the Neversink Mountain Railroad station, on the south face toward the Centennial Springs Hotel.

Rare interior view, showing the massive sitting room of the Neversink Mountain Hotel. The electric lighting was a novelty at the time. (Meiser- Passing Scene)

No Curb Service

Only two of the railway stations came close to the hotel- an early one on the north face called "Observation Point," and the other on the south face, which eventually became known as the Neversink Mountain Hotel stop, but which was quite a distance downhill. So in order not to inconvenience any of the guests with a walk of a few hundred yards, a horse and carriage would be sent to pick them up.

It must be remembered that the hotel was constructed after the railway was already in place. In order to take advantage of the spectacular view afforded by the easternmost peak of the mountain, the hotel would have to be built at a distance from any of the railway stops. Of course, this fit right in with the purpose of the hotel as a retreat, and the constant close passing of railway trolleys is something the patrons would have preferred to do without anyway.

A 14-foot wide piazza (porch, to us locals) surrounded the second floor. This deserves consideration- a walk around the piazza (a distance of more than 800 feet in all), could take quite a while.

The Neversink Mountain Hotel under construction in early 1892. Big crew for a big hotel. Note diagonal facing boards. (Meiser- Passing Scene)

The interior featured the latest in conveniences, including electric lights and bells, steam heat, hot and cold baths, and "pure" mountain spring water, which was piped up from the reservoir down the south face near Dengler's Glen Hotel.

The water was pumped up the hill in a pipe which was mostly above ground, "on account of hard digging" in the rocky terrain between the two hotels. This could have been a disaster in the winter, but was considered irrelevant, since the hotel would be closed during the winter anyway.

The water which reached the Neversink Mountain Hotel was stored in three large tanks, which were built inside the "towers" of the hotel.

Reality check: The sewer system for the Neversink Mountain Hotel drained down the south face of the mountain, toward Dengler's Glen Hotel. So the "pure" mountain spring water that was being piped up to the Neversink Mountain Hotel had only a few days before been urine and bathwater from above. Sorry to ruin your dinner here, but these are the facts, and codes enforcement is a relatively new idea.

Despite construction delays, due to difficult access for materials to the site, and a cost overrun of about 60,000 dollars, the Neversink Mountain Hotel opened in time for the tourist season of 1892, on July 7th.

It took a few years for the hotel to build up a clientele and there were only a few years when the hotel actually showed a "profit." But the profit was just on paper. Since the hotel had cost an additional $60,000 over what was initially capitalized by the investors, the profit was eaten up by the overruns. No investor ever received a dividend for his investment.

Part of the reason for the hotel's failure to make money was its short season- from June first until late fall. The rest of the year, it was a closed, empty liability, which needed to be heated despite the absence of visitors, to keep its pipes from freezing.

The hotel's elitism also hurt its profitability. Reading journalist Wayne Homan tells the story of local businessmen of the 1890s who would go up to the Neversink Mountain Hotel for dinner, and lounge on the breezy porch afterward.

After a few visits, these businessmen found that, by the time they had finished their meal, the chairs on the porch had been turned inward, and tilted toward the building. They got the message- local dinner customers were not appreciated.

After only ten years in business, it became evident that the hotel would never really live up to its promise for the investors. They were lucky if they broke even on their investment. Except perhaps for Mr. Merritt, whose company provided the massive amounts of lumber for the building project.

The mountain railway remained popular, and passengers continued to "ooh and aah" at Observation point. But fewer people were getting off at the Neversink Mountain hotel stop. After all, there WERE other resort hotels in the area, including The Woodvale Inn, down the hill in Mt. Penn.

Adjacent ads for the Neversink Mountain Hotel and the Woodvale Inn, in the same issue of the Neversink Item.
(Meiser- Passing Scene)

Hard Times

In 1903, as part of the P&R's massive sell-off on the mountain, (see the upcoming Klapperthal Pavilion Chapter), the Neversink Mountain Hotel was sold on the foreclosure of the mortgage to Heber Y. Yost, for $21,000. Yost was the secretary/treasurer of the Neversink Light, Heat and Power Company, which operated the power station on the Schuylkill which powered the railway. He also owned a few acres of land down the hill and to the west, near Hiener's Wissel, which he had acquired from the Klapperthal Company.

In the early days of the hotel, it was advertised as being open "until late fall." But by early fall in 1905, the hotel was already closed for the season, and there was only one employee on duty at the massive structure, which was seeing fewer visitors with each passing season.

Isaac Bowman was the watchman for the hotel on the night of September 29, 1905. About 8:30 p.m., Bowman noticed flames coming from the basement of the hotel, around the center. At around the same time, he saw flames at both ENDS of the structure- obviously arson.

The hotel's fire protection consisted of a few spigots with hoses attached, and ten fire extinguishers. As he struggled to find a way to put out the fire, the flames broke through the floor, and soon the west side of the hotel was an inferno.

Within ten minutes, the entire building was in flames. Watchman Bowman stated afterwards that he had "no doubt" that the fire was deliberate. Three strangers had been seen walking through the woods when the fire broke out, and the veranda was saturated with vast amounts of coal oil (kerosene).

Bowman, his wife, and their five year old daughter, who had been living in the hotel at the time of the blaze, escaped with nothing but the clothing they were wearing. After the fire, the Bowman family was put up in the Centennial Springs Hotel.

The fire was nothing short of spectacular, for the same reason that the view from the hotel had been spectacular. Messages were received by telephone and telegraph from as far away as 25 miles from people who could see the fire. Passengers on incoming trains could see the blaze.

In fact, the fire became a tourist attraction in its own right. The Neversink Mountain Railway, ever eager for business, put all of its cars into service that night, and delivered 1,500 passengers to the fire site between 9 p.m. and midnight of 9/29/05.

The "swinging bridge" at the P&R RR's Outer Station in Reading was a perfect vantage point for the fire, and was filled with so many gawkers that some feared it might collapse from the strain.

(Interesting note): Earlier on that very same day, September 29, 1905, Monsignor George Bornemann, who was the rector of St. Paul's Roman Catholic Church in Reading, and the founder of St. Joseph Hospital, had purchased the hotel property for $20,000, hoping to convert it into a retreat for nuns. This fact, according to historian George M. Meiser IX, was not immediately made known to the public.

Equally interesting is the fact that the property was insured for $31,250. Judging from the account in the Reading Eagle the next day, Mr. Meiser is correct. The account stated that the insurance, when collected, would be distributed among the hotel's bond holders. There was no mention of a sale the day before.

In fact, the Reading Eagle interviewed Mr. Yost the day after the fire. Yost declined to give the names of the current "owners," but speculated that the hotel would not be rebuilt.

Because of the resort's remote location, and the lack of water on the mountain top, the insurance had been hard to obtain, and had to be divided among 26 different companies, including Prussian National of Germany.

Today, there's barely a trace of what was once the largest and grandest hotel on Neversink. The site was located above 23rd Street in Mount Penn, at the highest and easternmost peak of the mountain.

Currently, the site is marked by the transmitting tower of WRFY/WRAW radio, surrounded by a chain link fence. In numerous hikes at the site, I have found bits of china that once bore the bounty served to visitors, which did include some locals, such as George Baer, George Brooke, and William H. Luden.

Early woodcut from a Reading, PA photo booklet. (Paul Druzba)

*Top: Early view from a photo booklet.
(Paul Druzba)
Bottom: Closed for the winter.
(Meiser: Echoes of Scholla)*

The McIlvain Pavilion

The resort does boast one survivor, though. The McIlvain Pavilion, a round, roofed brownstone structure still stands about 800 feet to the west of the hotel site, at the end of the oblong driveway that once encircled the hotel. The outline of the driveway is still very evident. The hotel's tennis court was located about halfway between the hotel and the pavilion.

William Mcilvain was president of the Second National Bank, president of the McIlvain Iron and Boiler Plate Company, the owner of a charcoal forge in Duncannon, Pa, and the owner of 2,000 wooded acres in Dauphin County. He was also a Foosgaenger.

Literally, from the German, foosgaenger is "foot walker", and the 100 members of the Berks County Foosgaengers, all men of wealth and power, shared a love of nature, and hiking.

McIlvain's favorite hike was along the north face of Neversink, from Heiner's Wissel to the Highland House and back. He and his foot walking (hiking) companions always made a point to stop at the eastern peak for a rest.

In 1892, two years after William McIlvain's death, his daughter Annie had a pavilion built in his honor, at the site where he and his fellow hikers would stop for a rest.

The pavilion was designed by Alexander Forbes Smith, noted local, kilt-wearing Scots architect who also designed a number of local churches and school buildings, the Baer building in Reading; also, quite a few of the structures in Penn's Common, including the original spring house, the stone wall entrance at 11th Street, and the bandstand (the original stone one, not the present Fireman's Memorial, which was built in the late 1930s.) There is another pavilion very similar to the McIlvain at Charles Evans Cemetery in Reading.

At the time of its construction, it was predicted that the pavilion would "last a century." It did indeed, and then some. And, if the mindless vandals who have plagued the pavilion for many years can be discouraged, it just might last another century.

The McIlvain Pavilion, and one of those newfangled automobiles.
(Meiser)

The Neversink Mountain Hotel was probably doomed from the start, for a number of reasons. The hotel's insistence on shunning local patronage was a disaster. Reading-area visitors and diners could have sustained the hotel in lean times, which came soon enough after the novelty of the hotel had worn off.

During the hotel's later years, proprietors were said to have regretted the fact that more local patrons were not seen. Despite this, and the expected resentment from locals for being shunned for more than ten years, The Reading Eagle reported after the fire that local people felt sorry that the hotel had not prospered, and had pointed to it with pride when visitors came to the area.

Competition was also a factor. Laborers building the Neversink Mountain Hotel could look down the hill toward another hotel being constructed just below- the Woodvale Mansion at 23rd Street and Fairview, at the junction of the East Reading and the Stony Creek Electric Railroads.

The lack of water on the mountaintop, despite the three tanks stored in the hotel's towers, was a fire hazard, which explains why insurance on the hotel was so difficult to come by.

Considering the size of the hotel, three water tanks, each eight feet wide and six feet deep, would not have had much of an impact on a big fire. In fact, a lake of water may not have rescued the hotel from deliberate arson. Exactly who was responsible for that arson will always be a subject for debate.

In fairness to the Monsignor, it should be noted that there was a plague of anti-Catholic sentiment around the turn of the 20th Century. A cathedral, which was built in Philadelphia around that time, (St. Paul's at Logan Circle) was designed with high windows, so that they wouldn't be the target of rock-throwing anti-Catholics.

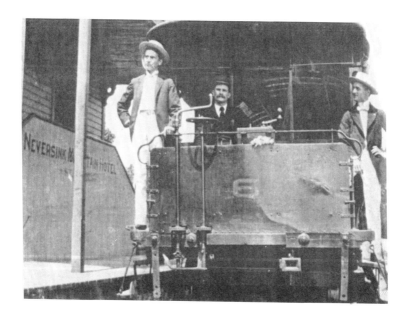

Car #6 stops at the Neversink Mountain Hotel.
(Reading: Points of Interest 1893)
Next page: Floor plan (Meiser: Passing Scene)

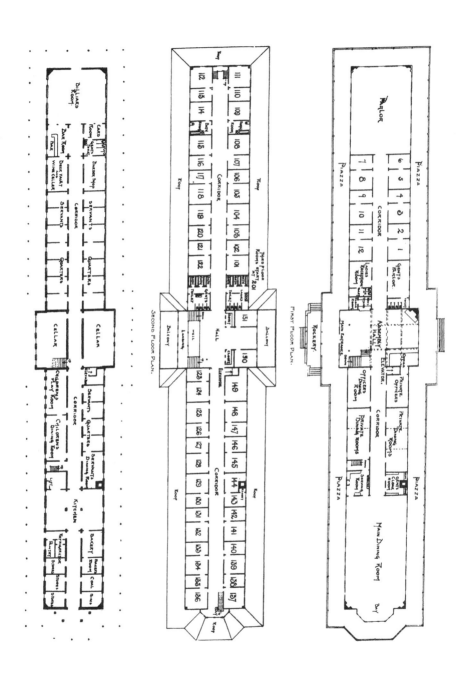

Young and old alike survey the remnants of the Neversink Mountain Hotel the day after the fire. Since nothing remains on the site except for some broken bits of china, it can only be assumed that the brick and stone were re-used for construction elsewhere.
(Meiser: Passing Scene)

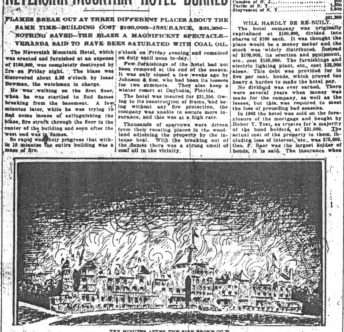

Reading Eagle account of the fire.

Chapter 6- Centennial Springs Hotel (Stop #5)

(Yes, I know, there are two "stop #5's." Read on, and you'll see why).

Moses K. Graeff, a Readingite/Readinger (would someone please clear this up!), once operated a "malt house" on South 9th Street in Reading. In fact, he and Frederick Schuldt began making malt in large quantities in 1863, and traded under the name of "Schuldt and Graeff" until 1867, when Mr. Schuldt retired. Graeff carried on the business until 1895, and most of the malt produced was shipped to Philadelphia and New York.

In the meantime, Graeff owned a 32-acre tract of land on the south side of Neversink Mountain, just above Klapperthal glen, which was once occupied by an old hermit who lived there in a log cabin. In August of 1890, Graeff complained to the Reading Eagle that there had once been a building on his land, but it was destroyed by "Hungarian laborers" who were grading the mountain for the railway. Could this have been the old hermit's log cabin?

(In the 21st Century, it seems odd to see a reference to "Hungarian workers" in a news story. However, in the 19th Century, the established residents of the area, mostly of German ancestry, were suspicious of and looked down upon recent immigrants, evidently forgetting that only a few generations before, their families had been immigrants themselves).

Graeff had been growing grapes on the tract, and planned to fit the place up as a "pleasure resort". Graeff said he would start building a two-story cottage late in August, and predicted that "within a few years, cottages will be erected all over the mountain." This prediction was partially fulfilled almost a century later.

He also stated that there would soon be a railway stop at his resort, a prediction that also only partly came true.

Graeff was an accomplished vintner, and his acres were much more sparsely populated by trees at that time, and turned out a very respectable crop of wine grapes along the hills above the glen. Mr. Graeff transported his grapes to "Renninger's in Stoney Creek" to be crushed, and the grape juice was brought back to be fermented in four huge barrels in the wine cellar, two on each side.

The Centennial Springs Hotel, larger than the hotel that Dengler had built lower in the glen, was probably named after the spring that ran along part of the property, which Graeff had acquired sometime around the Centennial of the United States, in 1876. It was also a hotel only in name at the beginning, although it did have a second floor. The upstairs was for the use of a tenant, who was put in charge of running the hotel downstairs.

The original portion of the hotel, on the lower part of the property, contained a wine cellar, where the wine was stored in racks suspended from the ceiling. Later, the original building was enlarged, and another building was built uphill from the original hotel.

It was reported that, in the peak of the tourist season (summer), The Centennial Springs Hotel's two buildings were full of lodgers, and the business did very well. This, despite the fact that the hotel never did get its own stop on the Neversink Mountain Railroad, although a rider could get fairly close by getting off at the Neversink Mountain Hotel stop. The slope was just too steep to alter the railway's route. Visitors would just have to walk the several hundred yards downhill to get to the Centennial Springs.

The hotel could also be accessed by way of a road that ran from South 19th Street, up and over the top of Neversink around where the McIlvain Pavilion stands, and down the other side to the Centennial Springs and on to Klapperthal.

Though beer was probably available at the Centennial Springs (how could you NOT have beer with a city of 13 breweries just over the hillside!), wine was the drink of choice at Graeff's hotel.

Graeff had been one of the investors in the Neversink Mountain hotel and, like the other investors, never made a penny off of it. Adding to his losses from the hotel up the hill, was the fact that The Centennial Springs suffered from relatively difficult access on the railway, and had much competition from the other hotels and their accompanying beer gardens, which were easier to get to.

The original structure of the Centennial Springs Hotel. This photo was taken in the afternoon, with the sun hitting the west side. To the right and below was, and still is, the wine cellar. (Meiser- Echoes of Scholla)

It is entirely possible that Graeff invested in the Neversink Mountain Hotel in the hope of gaining favor with the railroad, and perhaps getting a stop on the railway for his hotel. If he did, it didn't work.

The investment would have also made sense from a business point of view, because the Neversink Mountain Hotel, with its mainly out-of-town clientele, would not really have been competition for the Centennial Springs and its local wine-sipping patrons.

Moses Graeff died in 1906, and late in the year, his hotel went up on the auction block, which took place at the Union House, under the direction of auctioneer Thomas D. Becker.

The winning bidders were Edward E. Sweitzer and James O'Rourke, who paid $6,225 for the property. Their plan was to invest $10,000 in improvements, and open a new resort hotel. Sweitzer, whose name alone appears on the deed transfer, was primarily involved in quarrying, and acquired quite a few other properties around that same time. It is hard to say with certainty whether or not the hotel actually did re-open. It would seem, however, that it did, at least once.

In December of 1907, the Neversink Mountain Fruit and Vintage Company was chartered by Berks County. (Today, companies are registered with the State, but in those days, the County was responsible for chartering). At the top of the list of officers in the company was

Edward E. Sweitzer. A few months later, in February of 1908, the property was transferred from Sweitzer to the Neversink Mountain Fruit and Vintage Company.

The name of the company implies that its purpose was the picking, and probably also the processing into wine, of the many varieties of grapes on the property. There is no evidence of quarrying on the site to my knowledge.

A business card, acquired by the author in 2003, advertised the Grand Opening of the Centennial Springs Hotel on Neversink Mountain on Monday, May 17th, 1909. Whether this was the first or second attempt to re-open the hotel is unclear, and I couldn't verify from news accounts that it actually did happen. The only evidence is the business card.

> **GRAND OPENING**
> OF THE
> **Centennial Springs Hotel**
> NEVERSINK MOUNTAIN
> Monday, May 17th, 1909
> E. T. TEMPLIN, Prop.
> MUSIC BY BRASS BAND

(Paul Druzba)

Top: The later addition to the hotel. Note the open pavilion on the left. (Meiser)
Bottom: The hotel complex soon after acquisition by the Tuberculosis Society. Grape plantings can still be seen on left. (Meiser)

Tuberculosis Sanatorium

Meanwhile, in 1909, the local Cigar Makers Union tried to have one its members admitted to a hospital, with no success. The man was suffering from advanced tuberculosis- known at the time as "consumption", or "the white plague." The disease was poorly understood, and hospitals feared compounding the ills of their already-sick patients.

The Berks County Tuberculosis Aid Society was formed, for the purpose of raising $25,000 to build a local sanatorium, for the treatment of TB. Volunteers went door to door in Reading, at first meeting a cool reception.

In those days, a family member with tuberculosis was something you kept quiet. In addition to the disease being misunderstood, it was also seen as "poor people's disease"- resulting from dirty conditions and poor nutrition. And no self-respecting citizen wanted to be associated with that.

Tuberculosis was a serious ailment, often fatal, and was usually treated at a "sanitarium." The treatment at such a facility consisted mainly of "clean mountain air", a healthy diet, and rest.

In time the money was raised. That fall, the Neversink Mountain Fruit and Vintage Company sold the Centennial Springs property to the Society for $8,000. Sweitzer's use of the property in the few years he owned it may be unclear, but it's likely that the only money he might have made from it came from the grapes, and not the hotel.

In addition to the 30+ acres and 21 varieties of grapes that came with the property, the Tuberculosis Society received another bonus. Monsignor Bornemann, who was sympathetic to their cause, donated 15 additional acres which had been the grounds of the Neversink Mountain Hotel he had purchased in 1905.

The original building of the hotel had a bed capacity of 27, in 19 rooms. Prior to renovations by the Society, this building had one bath for the 19 rooms. The other building contained 20 rooms. After renovations and additions, the complex opened to the public in June, 1910, with a bed capacity of 57, and a considerable waiting list.

At the end of World War I in 1918, servicemen were admitted on an emergency basis, and by the following year, the majority of the beds were occupied by veterans. Several local people still remember relatives who stayed at the sanatorium. One had a sister who stayed there for a few months and was cured. Another told of a relation, a young girl of 17, who died there in the late 1920s.

(Note the two different spellings above. "Sanitarium" and "sanatorium" are often used interchangeably, but they are not quite the same thing. A sanitarium is basically a resort, where patients live in order to take advantage of ideal conditions, such as clean air or spring water. A sanatorium is a similar place, but one which also provides medical treatment. The Neversink facility was a sanatorium, in that it was staffed by nurses and at least one doctor who actually provided medical treatment. This could be compared to the difference between a psychologist and a psychiatrist).

In 1922, the County of Berks took over ownership and operation of the sanatorium, but by the late 20s, demand for beds exceeded supply, and the waiting list grew longer.

Berks voters approved a $450,000 bond issue for a new sanatorium in 1929, to be built in Bern Township. Despite the stock market crash and resulting depression, the new facility opened in 1932.

Once the patients from the Neversink Sanatorium had been moved to the new facility, the County began a search for buyers for the old facility. It was difficult, because of the stigma still associated with tuberculosis.

To make the facility more attractive, the County had it fumigated. Still no buyers. Finally, in the mid 30s, the buildings were torn down. For years afterwards, it is said, not a living thing was ever seen moving at the site of the former Centennial Springs hotel buildings and Sanatorium- the fumigators had done their job a little TOO well.

Today, much of the foundation of the original structure can still be seen. The wine cellar, which was in the rear (lower portion) of the original building, is still largely intact, complete with a hook where the racks of wine hung. Only the door is missing!

Right below the wine cellar is a small pond, which was built as an ice dam and reservoir for drinking water. At this writing, the concrete reservoir is still intact, and relatively easy to find over the winter when ground visibility is at its best.

NOTE: Contrary to at least one printed account, which stated that he had bought it as another possible retreat for nuns, Monsignor Bornemann in fact never owned the Centennial Springs Hotel.

Anna: A TB Story

In 1921, there were 900 reported cases of tuberculosis in Berks County. And there were 75 beds at the Berks County Tuberculosis Sanatorium on Neversink Mountain. If all those on the waiting list for treatment were lined up, they would have stretched all the way down to Dengler's Glen Hotel at Klapperthal.

One of the lucky ones in 1930 was an 8 year old girl from southeast Reading named Anna Moyer.

The doctor at her school noticed a cough, and a thin, frail body. Even though one of Anna's brothers had a "touch" of TB, Anna's was worse. Before long, she found herself in a strange bed, in a strange building on Neversink, sporting a very short haircut. (Lice were a problem at the TB Sanatorium).

Anna spent her first three months there confined to bed. Unlike her family down on South Third Street, Anna was well-fed, drank lots of milk, and enjoyed plenty of fresh air. Sound good?

It wasn't always. The fresh air was fine in the summer, but in winter, the windows were kept open. Hot, stuffy air was the enemy. The once-a-week Saturday bath was lukewarm or cold. The only time Anna ever got warm was at mealtime, when all patients ate at the dining hall together.

Anna was homesick, but visitors were infrequent, and few. Her family did not have a car, and the trolley did not run on Neversink any more. So they would have to take the Reading trolley up to 18th Street, and make the long trek up and over Neversink to see Anna.

Her family was struggling just to survive. Anna's dad was a fireman, but the City could not afford to pay him for a while during the Depression. So a local grocer, an Italian gentleman on South 4th Street, was kind enough to extend credit until payday arrived.

But life in the summer at the TB Sanatorium was better for Anna. Her "summer uniform" was short-shorts, high-top shoes and nothing else. (Older girls could wear a top). She could play ball with the handful of other children. There was a sandbox. And cherry trees to climb. And "sour grapes" outside- the legacy of a "Mr. Graeff". And Anna could walk over to the McIlvain Pavilion to take in a nice view of the City.

Anna was lucky to get in, and lucky to get out alive. A baby died while she was there, as well as a number of "older people". The TB kids watched with fascination as the corpses were taken to the morgue, right underneath where they slept. To a kid, this is something that happens to "other people, not you".

After eight months at the Sanatorium, Anna was set free- sort of. She returned home, but under orders. For the next two years, Anna was bused to an "Open Air School" in northeast Reading. There, on the top floor, the windows were <u>always</u> open, all year round, just like up on the hill.

Anna, and about 20 other TB kids, took third and fourth grade at Northeast. But she doesn't remember it as a hard time. "It was the depression- we were happy for what we had."

Anna ate well, and enjoyed a mid-day nap at school. And got well. And went on to marry a fella named Claude Wert.

Despite all the hardships, Anna considers herself lucky. We should all be so lucky to be able to feel that way.

Note: By the late 1930s, it was reported that the number of TB cases in Berks County had decreased dramatically. So by that time, the Sanatorium on Neversink probably would have been of sufficient size to handle the need. If the construction of Berks Heim had been delayed for a few more years, who knows? We might now see a sprawling care facility at the eastern end of Neversink Mountain. Another victim of changing times.

Left: Anna Moyer poses in summer garb at her temporary Neversink home. (Vallie Reich)
Right: Anna (far right) and some sick friends. "Our Gang"- 1930. (Anna Moyer Wert)

County Collection---Friday, November 19th, 1920
Neversink Mountain Tuberculosis Sanatorium

WE make our annual appeal to the people of Berks County for the Neversink Mountain Tuberculosis Sanatorium. We are co-operating with the United States Public Health Service in caring for soldiers who became victims of tuberculosis while serving our country in the World War.

In addition to taking the cure, the soldiers are using their leisure time in studying to fit themselves for some useful occupation after they are discharged as arrested cases. The Government Vocational Training Board has assigned two teachers as instructors and furnished the necessary equipment. The entire proceeds of the County Collection will be used to erect a building, suitable for educational, recreation and amusement purposes. We need about five thousand dollars. The Government pays for the maintenance of the soldier patients and all buildings and equipment becomes the property of the Sanatorium and will be used for our county patients, after the soldiers leave.

BERKS COUNTY TUBERCULOSIS SOCIETY

Full house of patients (mostly WWI servicemen) at the Sanatorium. Back of the card was a plea for donations. Note that the former pavilion on the left is now enclosed..
(Paul Druzba)

Left: Another "plea" card, issued to school students to take home to their parents. 1919. (Druzba)
Right: Present day remains of the reservoir just below (downhill from) the original hotel building. Still holds water, 100 years later! (Photo: Paul Druzba)

Chapter 7- Point Lookout (Stop #6)

Landscaping and view were the two big assets of Point Lookout, which was a brief stop along the Neversink Mountain Railway.

During construction of the railway, it was hard to miss the fact that this was one of the best views from Neversink Mountain, and perhaps one of the best in Pennsylvania.

Wrapping around the eastern summit of the mountain, the railway would backtrack west on the south side of the mountain, still on the ascent, toward the middle peak. Once the journey began a downhill path toward the middle peak, a spectacular view of the Schuylkill Valley unfolded.

The traveler could see southeastern Berks County for miles out over the valley, from the "Little Dam" near Poplar Neck to the Big Dam at Klapperthal. Riders who had only heard about the "Big S" formed by the Schuylkill could now see it first hand.

To make the view even more enjoyable, the railroad cut down any trees that might have obstructed that view, although there wouldn't have been that many anyway. Though the view is still pretty stunning in the 21st Century, some of it has become obscured by the growth of trees, which has gone unhindered since the mid 20th Century.

Again, beauty IS in the eye of the beholder. So, while it may seem a shame that the view could be better, the trees do have a beauty all their own.

There were a number of short "gawker" stops along the railway, but Point Lookout was the longest of these short stops. It would take a few minutes for the "oohs" and "ahhs" to subside, and by the turn of the 20th Century, those who had one of those new Kodak box cameras would have needed time to snap off a picture or two.

(In case you thought that the "disposable camera" was a recent idea, these early Kodaks were purchased pre-loaded with film, and when the film was exposed, the entire camera was sent out for processing, returning fully loaded again. Some things never change)

Note: The north face of this general area was also once known as "goat hill," because of a "watch goat," owned by the resident of the area. Old timers tell of "close encounters" with the nasty nanny goat, which was very protective of its owner's estate.

Ticket stubs for the Neversink Mountain Railroad. Though Lookout Point wasn't listed as a stop, cars routinely paused there for photos (Paul Druzba)

Chapter 8- Klapperthal Area

Before we tackle the various stops and attractions at Klapperthal, it's worthwhile exploring how the area got its name.

Today, the area generally referred to as "Klapperthal" encompasses a fairly <u>large</u> area, hundreds of acres, stretching along the lower slopes of the south face of Neversink from the bend in the present-day railroad tracks of the Philadelphia and Reading Railroad below Point Lookout, to the eastern limits of Neversink, ending in a cemetery in Exeter Township.

It's interesting and ironic that the area which provided inspiration for the name of Klapperthal, did not <u>acquire</u> the name. The reason reminds one of the old question, "If a tree falls in the forest and there's no one there to hear it, does it make a sound?"

In the days of the Civil War, an area at the western end of Neversink, just west of the area known as "Klapperthal Junction" and across from Poplar Neck, was a testing ground for cannon built in Berks County.

Since this part of Neversink was mainly devoid of trees at this time, and basically unpopulated except for a small farm or two, there was little fear of fire, or of bothering anyone.

The cannon testers built a huge pile of logs along the hillside to absorb the fire of the cannon. Most of the shells fired from what became for generations known as the "proving ground" hit their mark.

But occasionally, a round would ricochet off the pile of logs and careen over the mountain top, ending up in someone's backyard in Reading! One shot went through the roof of a man's shed on Haak Street in east Reading. The City would be unlikely to grant a permit for such activity today.

The tremendous noise of the cannons' firings would inspire the name of the area- Klapperthal, German for "thunder valley" or "clatter valley"- but, oddly enough, not in the area where the sound originated.

To the east, in Exeter Township, there was a fairly significant number of farms and homes, and the residents there could hear the loud echoes of the cannon, as the sound careened off the side of the mountain and thundered past their plows. It was these people, far to the east of the "proving ground" of the cannon, those most annoyed by the noise, who would have given Klapperthal its name.

If you look at charts and maps of Neversink, recent or old, you won't find a single reference to "Klapperthal" from Poplar Neck to the west. Yet, the proving ground where the cannon were fired was west of Poplar Neck.

Klapperthal Station, Klapperthal Pavilion and Klapperthal Park, not to mention the still-existing Klapperthal Road, Klapperthal Glen and Klapperthal Creek, are all well east of the proving ground site.

Note: Although the cannon proving grounds were mainly unpopulated, there was some farming going on there at the time. Earl Lincoln Ruppert related a story told by his grandparents, who lived near the proving grounds:

Ruppert's grandfather, Alfred G. Lincoln, was a foreman on the P&R. (Yes, they ARE descendants of Abe. Remember that the Lincoln Homestead is in Exeter Township).

Whenever Alfred's wife wanted to do some shopping in Reading, she would take a railroad handcar, and with the help of a few other nearby shoppers, would wheel the handcar down the tracks into Reading. When finished shopping, they would take the handcar back to the proving grounds.

The story also contains an account of a small boy, <u>unusually</u> small, who lived on a farm where Forest Hills Cemetery is now. The boy was so small that the cannon testers allegedly shoved him down the mouth of the cannon to clean the barrel, and inspect the interior. The fact that this occurred many years before the Child Labor Laws actually lends a measure of credibility to an otherwise outlandish tale.

Chapter 9- Klapperthal Park Station (Stop #8)

Klapperthal Park was a large area, encompassing hundreds of acres, from the area below Point Lookout, all the way to the eastern end of Neversink, beyond Klapperthal Glen.

Initially, the railway construction included Klapperthal Park, which was designed to be a place of natural beauty, and a great destination for a picnic.

To get there the railway built Klapperthal (Park) Station, at the eastern end of the big wooden trestle that carried passengers over Klapperthal Glen.

Klapperthal Park Station was an open air structure, like most of the stations on the Neversink Mountain Railroad, since it would only be used in warmer weather. It is often referred to as "Klapperthal Station", which is confusing, since the next stop on the railway was- Klapperthal Station!

Klapperthal Park at that time included some of the area now occupied by a cemetery fronting Neversink Road in Exeter Township.

If you imagine the Klapperthal part of the railway line resembling the head of a dinosaur (see map), the Klapperthal Park station was just to the right of the dinosaur's ear. If you were headed for a quiet picnic in Klapperthal Park, you would get off here, and walk down the steps into the beautiful glen below.

(If you stand on the wooden bridge which now crosses the pond and look toward Forest Hills Cemetery, the railway wound around in an arc about as far as you can see).

Klapperthal Park featured a large pond (or a small lake, if you like), the remnants of which can still be seen at the far end of Forest Hills Cemetery on Neversink Road in Exeter Township. The lake is now only a fraction of its original size.

Soon after the railway was completed, construction began on the railway's first giant gamble- Klapperthal Pavilion.

The lake at Klapperthal Park. (Meiser)

Top: Not a great photo technically, but the only known view of Klapperthal Park station showing its location- on the EAST side of the glen. (Handy Reference Railway Guide- 1902)
Bottom: Klapperthal Park station from the wooden trestle. (Meiser)

Top: Frank Suchomelly's boyhood home at Klapperthal, just below the nursery. @1930 (Frank Suchomelly)
Bottom: Late 1800's photo of "farmhouse at Klapperthal". Same area?. (Meiser)

Chapter 10-
Klapperthal Pavilion/
Klapperthal Station
(stop #9)

"Pavilion" is usually thought of as an open structure- a roof, held up by supporting posts- and a place to escape the rain and sun. But there is another definition, an architectural one, which describes the end of a facade, often treated as a tower. Though the common definition of pavilion applies to most pavilions that were built on Neversink, the architectural one seems more appropriate to Klapperthal Pavilion.

One of the largest and most-impressive-looking looking structures ever built on Neversink Mountain was the Klapperthal Pavilion. The brainchild of the Philadelphia and Reading Railroad, Klapperthal Pavilion was built early in 1892 to be a playground for visitors from Philadelphia, as well as Mountain Railway travelers from Reading.

A 300-foot long and 50-foot wide behemoth of brownstone and wood, the pavilion contained a bowling alley, shuffleboards, a huge bar, a banquet hall, smaller dining rooms, seating for 2,000, and one of the largest dance floors in Pennsylvania at the time.

The Pavilion, though slightly smaller than the Neversink Mountain Hotel, was still huge- as long as a football field. And it sported a cylindrical "tower" on its western end.

To run the establishment, the P&R hired the popular Reading restaurateur J.J. Kern. In late May of 1892, the Reading Press Club- dubbed "The Knights of the Lead Pencil" by the Berks and Schuylkill Journal, invited the management of the Neversink Mountain Railway, the Neversink Mountain Hotel Company, and the Mount Penn Gravity Railroad to a banquet at the Pavilion, which was mostly completed on the inside, but still needed lots of work on the outside.

(It is interesting, from a researcher's point of view, to note the William McIlvain was listed as one of the guests at the banquet, along with Morton McIlvain, William's son. William had actually died 18 months earlier!)

Before the festivities began, the entire party was treated to a short trolley ride up the mountain to the Neversink Mountain Hotel, which was then under construction and about a month away from opening.

Kern served up a sumptuous meal of sugar cured ham, Fulton Market tongue, and corned beef. Jesse G. Hawley served as toastmaster. The Press Club, which had been formed only five years before, had been doing its work quietly, but with this banquet, they hoped to let the community know who they were, and to identify the people who were helping the city's economy to grow.

The account of this banquet contradicts and disproves a later account by the Reading Eagle in 1903, which reported that the Pavilion had been built in 1894.

Kern was replaced in 1894 by 40 year old Augustus B. Hassler of Reading, who had retired from the hotel business a year before. Hassler ran the Pavilion for a year, and later became proprietor of the Germania Hotel at Ninth and Penn Streets in Reading, where travelers used to board trolleys to the mountain from Reading.

Klapperthal Pavilion was located "just" behind Klapperthal Station, a P&R RR stop in the valley between bends of the Schuylkill River.

In reality, Klapperthal Pavilion was located a few hundred yards uphill from Klapperthal Station, and on a slight plateau before a dramatic rise up the south face of Neversink. The plateau was flat enough, in fact, to accommodate a baseball field, which was very popular on Sundays, because it was then illegal to play "base ball" in Reading on Sundays. The pavilion was located in Cumru township, and not in the City of Reading.

The Pavilion grounds, comprising nine acres, also featured croquet, swings, and a roller coaster- which, like the one at the Highland House, lasted only for one year.

Some Reading companies held their picnics at Klapperthal Park and Pavilion. One such picnic, for the Reading Hardware Beneficial Association, was held on August 27, 1892. The picnic, reported on in the following week's Berks and Schuylkill Journal, drew an amazing crowd of 10,000 people, the largest ever at the Pavilion! On that day, the Germania Band performed in the Pavilion, and the Ringgold Band over in the Glen. Observers in Reading noted how unusually empty the streets were that day. The dance floor of the pavilion was so crowded that dancing was difficult.

Heavy, metal pendants (they were called "badges") were distributed for the event as souvenirs. I am the proud owner of one of them. My badge has special meaning to me, since my father once worked at Reading Hardware, although he wouldn't be born until 30 years after this particular picnic. It's a telling statistic: the largest crowd ever assembled at Klapperthal Pavilion was in its first year of operation.

WHICH Klapperthal Station?

Klapperthal Station, not to be confused with Klapperthal Park Station, was built specifically to deliver passengers of the Philadelphia and Reading Railroad, as well as passengers of the Neversink Mountain Railroad, to Klapperthal Pavilion and Park.

Neversink Mountain Railroad cars came into the station on one of two spurs, just a few feet north of the P&R tracks. Since there was no place for the cars to turn around, the seats were reversed (a la the White House Hotel stop) for the return trip.

Klapperthal Station, serving both the P&R RR and the Neversink Mountain Railroad. (Meiser)

Top: Klapperthal Pavilion from across the Big Dam. Note the water level at the tunnel.
(Meiser)
Bottom: A P&R train passes the Pavilion. This is not a trick photo. The pavilion was HUGE!
(Meiser)

Short-Lived Fun

The various attractions of Klapperthal Pavilion and its surrounding Park drew visitors from near and far, but in dwindling numbers each year, until about 1902.

Novelty has a way of making people endure, and even enjoy, dumb ideas. It took a few years for visitors to realize that, despite the many attractions at Klapperthal Pavilion, the air in that part of Neversink is very still, with breezes cut off by the mountain. This made a hot summer day unbearable in the Klapperthal Pavilion area in the days before air conditioning.

In addition to the less than perfect weather, embarkers at Klapperthal Station also had a bit of an uphill walk to Klapperthal Pavilion. (This was typical of a number of stops along the Neversink Mountain Railway. The terrain limited how close the railway could get to the site.)

Due to declining patronage, Klapperthal Pavilion was abandoned. George Baer, now President of the Pennsylvania and Reading Railroad, had little patience for ventures that did not make money.

The Pavilion was not the only attraction on Neversink which was suffering from declining patronage. Around the same time, the railroad's other venture, the Neversink Mountain Hotel, was sold. Just a few years before, the Neversink Mountain Railway had been put up for sheriff's sale.

The novelty of the railway and its surrounding attractions had obviously worn off, and it became evident that maintenance costs would make future profit impossible, not only from the railway, but also from the resort attractions that the railway serviced.

In February, 1903, the Philadelphia and Reading Railroad sold the pavilion, lock stock and barrel, to James R. Kline of Monocacy for an undisclosed price. No doubt it was a small fraction of what the railroad had paid to build it.

Klapperthal Pavilion in its prime.
(Meiser)

The Pavilion Lives On!

Mr. Kline was determined to get the most for his money in his purchase of the pavilion. None of the materials were wasted!

The materials list from the sale included 3,000 yards of red dressed sandstone (brownstone), 1,000 yards of well-faced sandstone, 18,000 feet of sheeting, 24,000 feet of rafters, 18,000 feet of yellow pine flooring, 60,000 feet of hemlock lumber, and 35,000 shingles. Also included were three refrigerators, a 48-foot bar, 20 tables, 1,000 feet of underground piping, and a range that was 30-feet long!

Morris Romig, who was renting the Klapperthal farm at the time (where the very small cannon cleaner boy came from, and later the site of Forest Hills Cemetery), acquired the sandstone (presumably from Mr. Kline).

Romig built a beautiful home with it on the corner of what is now Romig Avenue and Neversink Road in Reiffton, not far from the site of the former Pavilion. The home still stands, and is still very impressive.

When Romig's house was finished, he sold the remainder of the stone to William Hafer, who built a large farmhouse with it at the "lower end" of Neversink Road. Who knows what became of the piping, not to mention the 48-foot bar!

At least some of the lumber from the Pavilion ended up in the hands of Frank Bechtel, a contractor in the Exeter area. Bechtel used the lumber to build at least five homes on Neversink Road, just south of the entrance to Forest Hills Cemetery.

Frank Suchomelly showed me the floor boards and joists of his first floor, which were once part of the Klapperthal Pavilion. Bechtel was, coincidentally, the grandfather of Frank Suchomelly's wife, Cora.

Today, despite our apparent emphasis on recycling, torn-down buildings are often landfilled. In fact, what was once a deep depression on the south side of Neversink is now filled with the remains of many of the buildings which were torn down in Reading throughout the 20th Century, and that landfilling continues today.

The railroad may have been fabulously wealthy at the turn of the 20th Century, but the residents of the Klapperthal area were not, and quickly seized on the leftover materials of a Railroad misjudgement.

Although there are reports of a circular foundation of a water storage facility at the site of the former Pavilion, no other traces of the structure have ever been found, and exploring is now difficult in what was once an open field, but is now a thick overgrowth of woods and brush.. The buyers evidently left little on the site to intrigue future historical explorers.

Note: During its "boom" period, the railroad spent lavish amounts of money on the Pavilion, the railway, and the mountain in general, with little thought of risk. But revenues fell short of expectations, and the replacement of the railroad by the next dominant form of transportation, the automobile, returned the mountain to its former state of anonymity.

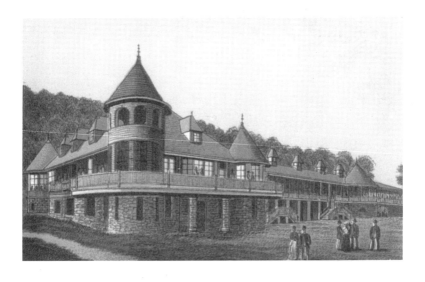

Early woodcut of the Pavilion, from a souvenir booklet published by Reading stationer J. George Hintz.
(Paul Druzba)

Chapter 11- Dengler's Glen Hotel- The Last Resort? (Stop #8-A)

Another popular getaway on Neversink Mountain in the "Gay 90s" (another term which has taken on a different meaning since then) was Dengler's Glen Hotel, built in 1892 by Charles Dengler, one of the Mount Penn Denglers from the other side of Neversink. "Old Timers" refer to it as Dengler's Glen Hotel, The Glen Hotel, the Glen Inn, and the Glen Valley Hotel. See what happens when you don't put up a sign?

Dengler's hotel was designed to be a retreat for hard working people looking for a little relaxation in a quiet setting. In fact, now that the railway no longer thunders over the wooden trestle nearby, and the clatter of horse-drawn carriages are no more, and cars can no longer negotiate the road, the site of the former Glen Hotel is one of the quietest spots in Berks County- literally!

Situated in Klapperthal Glen, between the pond at the rear of Forest Hills Cemetery and the remains of the Centennial Springs Hotel, Dengler's Glen Hotel had a credible claim to being the quietest resort on Neversink. It was situated in an area which drops off drastically from the level of the surrounding hills, and is shielded from most of the noise of the city and present-day highways. It's nothing short of eerie how quiet the place is! You really can hear a pin drop!

The area is thick with Pennsylvania's state flower, the Mountain Laurel, which is a slow-growing evergreen shrub, and is a sight to behold in June.

Earl Ruppert, in his writings for the Exeter anniversary booklet in 1968, remembered that the Glen Hotel had "a large dance pavilion." During the summer, a 'Mr. Garmon' held dances there on Wednesday and Saturday evenings." This dance pavilion appears to be the same one that had once graced the property of the Highland House. Dengler apparently bought it from the ailing Highland House in the 19-teens, and arranged to have it sent down to the glen piecemeal on the railway.

Frank Suchomelly, a Maryland native whose family moved to the Klapperthal area in 1922 when he was four years old, had many memories of the Glen Hotel. His mother Katherine (Katrina in the original German) worked as a cook at the hotel in the late 1920s.

Like the White House, the Glen Hotel made no pretenses of being a proper "hotel." There were no rooms to rent. It was basically a bar, with food served for bar patrons. Frank's mother worked mostly weekends, when the bar was busiest, preparing "traditional German dishes," especially chicken.

The proprietor, Charles Dengler (who Suchomelly refers to as "Oscar,") and his wife Maggie, were known to the locals as "Maggie and Jigs" (after cartoon characters of the day). Charles Dengler also maintained a vineyard along the rising slopes of the Neversink to the west of the hotel, as did his uphill neighbor, Moses Graeff. If you visit the site now it's hard to imagine, but at the time, there were virtually no trees in the area, so a vineyard is easier to visualize in those circumstances.

On the north side of the hotel site was a small fish pond, the outline of which can still be seen at the site, and which was optimistically referred to as "Mirror Lake." The base for one of the fence posts surrounding the pond remains.

Along the eastern bank of the Glen Hotel area was a chicken house. The chickens were served for dinner at the hotel, or sold to locals.

The secluded area of the glen was also the scene, in the 1890s, of several murders and/or suicides. It is reported that several jealous or jilted lovers, who met at the Klapperthal Pavilion, met their end in the glen.

Dengler's Glen Hotel, which was originally meant as a "watering hole" for locals, must have been seen as having greater possibilities by the mid 1890s. Witnessing the construction of the railway trestle just to the south of his hotel, Dengler must have figured he could gain more customers from the tourists who were traveling the Neversink Mountain Railway.

Top: Dengler's Glen Hotel, late 1890s.
Bottom: The dance hall behind the Glen Hotel,
formerly at the Highland House. @1900
(Both photos- Meiser: Echoes of Scholla)

In 1896, Charles Dengler paid the Neversink Mountain Railway the sum of $1,000 to build a spur line, connecting nearby Klapperthal Park, (which had a Railway stop of its own) to Dengler's Glen Hotel. Klapperthal Park Station, which had originally been the first stop on "the short line" of the Railway, was now one of two options when one reached the Glen.

The spur to Dengler's broke off on a curve at the point where the big trestle began over the gorge and creek below, and the spur line actually required a number of smaller wooden trestles to accommodate the creek on its way up to Dengler's Glen hotel.

Later, when the P&R abandoned Klapperthal Pavilion and the Neversink Mountain Railroad, the line from Klapperthal Park Station down to Klapperthal Station was closed, and Dengler's became the "terminus" of the railway, since there was no longer any reason to travel any farther on the original line.

Though just a young boy at the time, Frank Suchomelly also helped out over at Klapperthal. The pond below Dengler's hotel had a healthy supply of frogs, and Frank remembers catching frogs from the pond and taking them up to the hotel, to be served later for dinner. Suchomelly also carried spring water in buckets down the trail along Klapperthal Creek to the Neversink Power House by the Schuylkill, to the thirsty workman inside.

*Top: A NMR car awaits passengers at "The Terminus". Glen Hotel in background. (Druzba)
Bottom: A view of Dengler's Glen, mislabeled as the Summit House on Mount Penn.
(Corrie Crupi)*

The Klapperthal Bear

Arthur D. Graeff, co-author of "Echoes of Scholla" with George M. Meiser IX, relates a story told to him by Raymond E. Kiebach, regarding the incident of the "Klapperthal Bear":

In the fall of 1902, it is reported that an Italian gentleman with a trained bear was giving a performance at a hotel in Mount Penn, most probably the Woodvale or the Black Bear. After the performance, the bear was tied up to a hitching post while the owner went in to collect his fee.

At that moment, a misguided thief absconded with the bear, and headed off over Neversink Mountain, ending up at the Glen Hotel. There, he tried in vain to persuade the bear to dance for the Glen audience. When the bear refused, the man made the severe misjudgment of cuffing the bear, which soon had the poor unfortunate pretender pinned to the floor.

The then-current proprietor of the Glen, "Newt" Keene, fired his revolver from the second floor to try to scare off the bear, but to no avail. Fortunately for the Johnny-come-lately bear trainer, the deaf-mute son of Moses Graeff, the owner of the nearby Centennial Springs Hotel, came to the rescue. The son, who because of his affliction could not have been intimidated by the growl of the bear, calmly gathered up the beast and tied it to a tree.

Soon afterward, the Italian gentleman was seen scurrying down the hill into the glen, apparently armed, shouting, "You shoot bear, I shoot." The REAL bear trainer indignantly marched off with his furry friend and dinner ticket, and the unfortunate pretender, now mauled, was taken to a hospital in Reading.

Mr. Kiebach, the relater of this story, heard it from his father, who resided at a house on Neversink Road where the Glen Hotel proprietor stopped on his way back from the hospital after delivering the beaten-up bear thief.

A "reverse" painting, which hung in the Glen Hotel until the late 1920s.
(Frank Suchomelly- Photo: Paul Druzba)

Another Speakeasy

Prohibition, which began in 1920, had put pressure on any easily accessible establishment serving alcohol. The Glen Hotel, as well as the Highland House, because of their remote locations, continued to thrive as speakeasy's during Prohibition.

A Birdsboro area historian, Bruce Hoffman, tells the tale of his father, a Birdsboro druggist, who used to rap on the door of the Glen Hotel in the late 20s, and give a greeting, something like "Joe sent me," to be let in. (In his younger days, Bruce's father was not allowed to ride the Neversink Railway by HIS parents, who said it was too dangerous).

The Neversink Mountain Railroad had ceased operations in 1917, and the trestle which spanned the Glen was removed in the mid 1920s. Locals, such as Mr. Hoffman, would continue to access the Glen Hotel via Klapperthal Road in Exeter.

Business would have reverted back to mainly local patrons, mostly from the Exeter and Birdsboro areas. This probably remained steady until the big stock market crash of 1929, after which most people were out of work. By 1930, police or no police, business at the Glen Hotel must have dried up to a trickle.

Another Fire

The Glen Hotel burned very early in the morning of September 27th, 1931. According to Suchomelly, the Reiffton Fire Company arrived too late to be able to control the fire, so they let it burn out. At the time of the fire, there was some talk in the neighborhood of arson, and insurance.

The fire destroyed the hotel in a hurry. Other buildings, including a dance hall, were eventually removed. The only things remaining today on the site of the Glen Hotel are some stone foundations, in one of the quietest spots in Berks.

As with any archeological site (and it IS an archeological site until someone destroys it), the foundation belies the size of the original structure. Looking at the foundation today, it's hard to imagine anything but a small shed on top of it. But if you look at a photo, and take away the porches and the overhanging roofs, it's easier to see the actual size of the hotel.

Also surviving from the Glen Hotel are a few "reverse paintings," which were done by a "Reading area" artist around 1890. These paintings were painted directly on the glass, which would be later framed.

From a painter's point of view, reverse paintings are difficult to do, because the "highlights" have to be done first, rather than last, probably with the use of a mirror, so they would show through the glass in proper perspective.

Frank Suchomelly still has two of these paintings hanging in his bedroom on Neversink Road, which he acquired over generations from his mother working at the Glen Hotel.

An open car with "cow catcher" on the front prepares for departure from the Glen Hotel terminus. Female passengers are in their Sunday finest. (Druzba)

Part 7- Random Notes on Neversink

Quarries

In addition to the ochre mine mentioned earlier, there was also a stone/sand quarry on the north face, above 20th Street, along the road which was later used to access the Berks County Sanitarium.

The quarry was owned by Al Mertz, who around 1900 furnished the stone that was used to build the greenhouse in City Park.

I know this sounds confusing to an out-of-towner, but City Park was only called "City Park" after 1900. Before that time, for more than a hundred years, the area was commonly known as "Penn's Common."

Around 1980, signs reading "Penn's Common" were installed around the park in an effort to reaffirm the park's original identity. The effort seems to have failed, and City Park is still the most common title. Old habits die hard.

Junked Cars and Narrow Trails

As of the turn of the 21st Century, there are still a number of junked cars scattered around Neversink Mountain, mostly vintage 1960s. Yes, they are ugly, and hopefully they will be removed soon. But many hikers who encounter one marvel at how a car could have gotten to such a remote location in the first place. But it must be remembered that the same natural forces that restored the greenery on Neversink, as well as some unnatural ones, also washed away some of the handiwork of the builders of the railway. Long, flat trails that seem much too narrow to carry a 40-passenger trolley car were once wider, and have been narrowed by erosion from a century of rain, motorcycles and fire.

Oil Wells?

In the early 1900s, an unnamed enterprising soul built an oil derrick near Klapperthal Park, just inside the circle where the railway extended into what is now Forest Hills Cemetery.

This disingenuous young man actually sold shares in what was promoted as being an oil well on Neversink! He went so far as to bury a drum of oil, poked full of holes, in Klapperthal Creek, to give the appearance of oil in the area.

Of course, no oil was ever pumped from this "well," which once stood on a slope very near to the present grave of local baseball great Carl Furillo, Jr. Locals remember the incident very well, but no one is sure exactly how much money this man bilked from his oil well "investors," or how much time he did; but he did get caught.

"Oil well" at Klapperthal? Not really. But impressive enough to prove that P.T. Barnum was right. (Meiser: Echoes of Scholla)

Property Lines?

Exactly who owns what on Neversink is sometimes a little hard to determine. It seems that when the Klapperthal Company acquired the necessary land on Neversink for the railway, the deeds were not very specific. This would have been George Baer's area of expertise.

Areas which included the railway beds for the Neversink Mountain Railroad were especially fuzzy, and, according to the Berks County Conservancy, would be difficult to verify in the 21st Century, and might take years.

A Place Called "Neversink?"

The name "Neversink" has been attached to many places and things. There was the Neversink Fire Company, way down in the valley below at Third and Court Streets. There was the Neversink Gun Club, on Painted Sky Road in Exeter Township, a few miles from the eastern foothills of the mountain. And there were businesses, like Neversink Spas, and the now-defunct Neversink Brewery, which were not really near Neversink Mountain at all.

But it is generally accepted that the area where Frank Suchomelly grew up was once referred to as Neversink.

In 1914, a brick school building was built, replacing an earlier wooden one, just beside an overpass of the present West Shore Bypass in Exeter, near the P&R Railroad tracks. This was known as Neversink School.

Frank attended Neversink School, and remembers the Neversink Station of the P&R Railroad which was only a few hundred feet to the south of the school. This was the last station on the P&R, at Klapperthal, before a westbound train would reach Klapperthal Junction, which was not at Klapperthal.

Suchomelly remembers the building eventually becoming the Artists Casino lounge, and later Bully Lyons Restaurant (named after an especially colorful character in Berks history).

Bully Lyons Restaurant later became the "Texas" saloon, and burned to the ground in 1988, just a few years after I had an excellent lunch there. It is now the site of a private home which sits a bit farther back on the lot than the original school and restaurant.

Suchomelly, who lives only a few hundred yards up the hill from the site, remembered selling bricks from the burned restaurant for "$10 apiece."

Artists Casino Restaurant at Neversink in early 1950s. Later Bully Lyons, later Texas. Formerly Neversink School.
(Paul Druzba)

What is a "hotel?"

In the late 19th Century, and lasting until the present, the term "hotel" in Berks County has been rather flexible. The same goes for the terms "Inn" and "Pavilion."

Many "hotels" in Berks started out as places to rest up for the night, but the rooms were later abandoned, and the establishments were scaled down simply to a bar or restaurant.

Good examples are the "Rising Sun Hotel" in Reading, and the Yellow House Hotel in Yellow House, which now also serves as a B&B. (Exeter Township).

Later, establishments that were meant strictly as a bar or restaurant adopted the name "hotel." So it should never be assumed, especially in 19th Century Berks County, that a "hotel" actually had rooms to let.

George Baer Highlights

A great man can be an important influence on history, especially if he has some influence over the historian.

George Baer, whose role in at least three different companies in the creation of the Neversink Mountain Railroad is well documented, is featured prominently in Morton

Montgomery's two-volume history of Berks County.

Less than earth-shattering accomplishments, such as being a member of the Board of Park Commissioners, and a member of Second Reformed Church, are mentioned. But not a word about the failed railway can be found in his biography in the work. Odd.

George Baer portrait, which now hangs in the Hendel Mansion on Centre Avenue, an annex of the Historical Society of Berks County. (Photo: Paul Druzba)

Reservoir

For a "baby boomer" such as myself, no account of Neversink would be complete without at least a mention of the reservoir. Yes, I know that it dates beyond the end of the resort period, but indulge me.

Back around 1960, I used to play football with some buddies up at the reservoir, which is a flat spot on the western end of Neversink, about the size of a softball field, about 2/3 of the way up the hill from 10th and South playground. We knew it as the "reservoir" even though none of us had ever seen any water there.

The Neversink Reservoir was built in 1936, on just over 29 acres of land, which was acquired by the city in 1865 for $890. The cost of construction, including fixing the initial leaks, was $202,000. That's a good chunk of change, considering that it was built during the Depression when labor was still cheap. Still, the maintenance costs for the first year amounted to a meager $282, including 75 cents for grounds care. (See what I mean about "cheap labor"?)

While some earlier reservoirs in Reading (most notably City Park) started out being open to the air, and later covered over, the Neversink reservoir was covered right from the start. (Just imagine what a chore it would be to clear the leaves out of an open air reservoir in the woods on Neversink! An open air reservoir would also require the services of a watchman, which the Neversink Reservoir actually had initially, despite the fact that it was covered. The watchman accounted for all but two dollars of the 1936 maintenance costs.)

The bottom of the structure is 26 feet below the surface. It's about 260 feet square, made of concrete, and contains just over 19 feet of fresh water when it's full, which is mainly in the evening when demand is low. The top of the reservoir is held up by huge concrete pillars, making the inside look like an ancient temple.

The water is piped in from the Maidencreek watershed, and when full, contains 9.92 million gallons of water. The reservoir is still very much in use, and supplies east Reading with its drinking water.

Every so often the Water Authority, which leases the reservoir from the City, sends a team of divers down to inspect the facility. On the last inspection, the divers also boarded rafts to inspect the ceiling. According to Tony Consentino, Executive Director of the Reading Water Authority in 2002, the Neversink reservoir is still in "very good shape."

The reservoir could have eased most of the water problems during Neversink's "resort years" had it been built about 50 years sooner. But again, not even a lake would have prevented destruction by arson.

Interior of the Neversink Reservoir at its completion in 1936. Resembles a Greek temple. (Historical Society of Berks County)

NOTE: It's amazing how many people think that concrete is a recent invention. The truth is, the Romans perfected the use of concrete several millennia ago. But when Rome fell, the recipe was lost.
"Modern" engineers began to "discover" it again about 150 years ago, and it was once again "perfected" early in the 20th Century. It pays to write down recipes.

Q- Who Lives in the White House?
A- Drobek!

This popular Q&A, first told to me by my uncle Luke Lubas from the days when he and his brothers would walk along the western end of Neversink, was also popular among the German, Polish and Irish immigrants in the bars at the foot of Neversink near 10th and South in the 1930s. It was an east Reading "inside joke," and very indicative of the "melting pot" that was Reading over the past 100 years, and continues today.

(I am not an insensitive person. I realize that you have been waiting for more than 100 pages for the answer to the question about which hotel on Neversink was the last one standing, and your wait is about to be rewarded. But first, the Drobek story.)

According to Carl Drobek, Jr., there was an Italian gentleman named "de Angelo" from Millmont who had applied for his citizenship papers in the early years of the Depression. Appearing before Judge Mays, de Angelo was asked, "Who lives in the White House?" Without hesitation, de Angelo replied, "Drobek."

The judge smiled and said, "Well, that may be true in Reading, but who lives in the White House in Washington?" De Angelo replied, "El Presidente," and thereby earned his citizenship.

The "Drobek" that this new American referred to was Carl's father, Carl Drobek Sr., who lived with his wife Maryann and their six children in the White House Hotel in the early 1930s.

The Drobeks had no intention of operating a hotel at the White House. They were in the bottling business. Carl Sr. had owned a bottling works on South 9th Street, but it burned down in the late 1920s. So when the White House hotel and bottling works became available, the Drobeks bought it, and moved their family of eight into the former hotel.

Carl Jr., described the hotel/home of his youth as "very nice, with thirteen rooms, and a dance floor." The Drobeks tried to earn a living with the bottling works across the Whitehouse Road, bottling spring water from Neversink, and a variety of sodas, including birch beer (a Berks County staple) and various fruit flavors.

But the spring was drying up, and they faced stiff competition from other bottlers. "It cost us 24 cents to bottle a case of soda, 24 bottles," recalls Drobek Jr. "Frank's of Philadelphia was selling theirs for 25 cents a case. We just couldn't compete."

In addition, financial problems caused by a dishonest employee at Free Savings and Loan at 9th and Bingaman were causing some problems with the Drobeks' creditors. Finally, by about 1932, Drobek threw in the towel, and sold the business to Dr. Thaddeus Matuszak, whose son-in-law was also in the bottling business.

The drying spring got drier, and Matuszak soon sold out to yet another competitor, a company from Philadelphia. They too had no interest in the hotel, or even in bottling on Neversink Mountain with its dried-up spring. The company's only interest was in the bottling equipment, which they promptly cleared out from the bottling works, and abandoned the property. That's when the scavengers moved in.

Recycling building materials was a long-standing tradition on Neversink, and it was no different with the White House hotel. Once the locals realized that the Philadelphia company wasn't interested in the buildings, they helped themselves.

By 1934, barely a trace of the hotel was left, and only the foundations of the bottling works. So, here's the answer to the question posed earlier: The <u>oldest</u> hotel on Neversink Mountain was also <u>the last to stand</u>.

The White House Hotel, built around 1840 (more than 40 years before its nearest competitor) lasted almost 100 years, at least two years later than the Glen Hotel. Ironically, The White House, which had sprung up long before the Neversink Mountain Railroad, proved to outlast it and all of its endeavors. The only structure on Neversink to last longer has been the McIlvain Pavilion.

Neversink Postscript: Ironic Demise

Daniel H. Christian was an Exeter Township native, and a very talented man. Working on various projects for the Philadelphia and Reading Railroad, including the Manayunk Tunnel, Christian rose rapidly in the ranks of the P&R RR. Christian came to be recognized as an expert in curved track-laying, and electrical work.

He supervised construction of the Neversink Mountain Railroad power station at the Big Dam, eventually becoming Superintendent of the Railroad. As such, he invented a brake shoe that was used on the Neversink Railroad, and a fender, which was used on Reading and Philadelphia Traction Company cars. He also invented an automatic block signal and an automatic switch.

Due to his status as an electrical wizard, Christian was put in charge of all electrical work on the Neversink Railway, and remained in that position when the Railway was sold to the Reading Traction Company in 1903.

But one can never be too careful. In that same year, 1903, Christian was fatally electrocuted while changing a light bulb at the Reading Traction Company car yard in Reading.

Part 8- Traces and A Look Ahead

Taking a stroll along Neversink today, you'd find precious little evidence of the activity that transformed the mountain 100 years ago, from a tranquil farming and open area, to a bustling, clattering resort community.

Today, the woods look virginal (except for the occasional wall, foundation, bag of trash, or junked car)- a tribute to what nature can do to heal the scars and cover the traces of man's handiwork. What the mountain <u>should</u> look like is, of course, a matter of opinion, and changes with time.

In his 1925 history, "The Story of Berks County," F.W. Balthaser gushed of "wonderful changes" that had occurred since the time of the Lenni Lenape. One of the "wonderful changes" he spoke of was that "most of the forests have been cut down."

He wasn't being sarcastic- he really believed that forests were a nuisance, and needed to be cleared in the name of "Progress". And the people who developed Neversink Mountain in the late 19th Century felt essentially the same. In case you're thinking that people are more enlightened now, consider this: the judge who created the "bald spot" at the site of the former Highland House in the latter part of the 20th Century, proves that things haven't changed much. Yes, we're outraged, but the bald spot is still there.

(To its credit, the Historical Society of Berks County reprinted the Balthaser book in 2002, in honor of Berks County's 250th anniversary, in its entirety, complete with all of its "politically-incorrect" references, including the one mentioned above).

But, even though the mountain has regained much of its original appearance, if you take a close look today, you can still see a few signs of times past on Neversink- a time of seemingly limitless growth and prosperity, speculation and optimism, and in some cases, poor judgment.

Today, before a construction project is begun, there are seemingly endless studies done, including environmental studies, soil and perk testing, and feasibility studies- including access to water and other necessities.

If any of these had been done in the 1890s, odds are there would have been few attempts at developing Neversink Mountain. Geology, weather, and changing times all conspired to doom enterprise on Neversink.

History and experience have shown that the danger of fire on Neversink is extreme and hard to control. And access to the mountain remains difficult and slow. The soil is too porous to hold water long enough for successful agriculture except in the most rainy season imaginable. (Exceptions are the relatively lush "glen" area, and the area called the "proving grounds," which supported farmers for generations.

So what does the future hold for Reading's "other' mountain?" Hopefully, from a developer's point of view, not much. Today, hikers take to the hills of Neversink in increasing numbers, to enjoy its beauty, which has largely returned to its natural state.

But before you put on your hiking shoes, it's important to remember that Neversink is still a patchwork of land parcels, some owned more or less publicly, and some privately. There are people living on the mountain who would rather not share their back yard with strangers.

Tunnel?

In the mid 20s, serious consideration was being given for a tunnel, to be bored through Neversink Mountain in the vicinity of Klapperthal. Fortunately, it never came to pass.

The Berks County Conservancy

A local, non-profit organization committed to preserving farmland and open space in Berks County, The Berks County Conservancy has been working for more than 10 years, acquiring land for preservation on Neversink. At this writing, the Conservancy currently owns about 300 acres of land on Neversink, with easements totaling another 35 acres. An easement is an agreement with a property owner which allows a portion of a property to be used for public purposes within certain limits.

The County of Berks and the City of Reading also own about 200 acres of Neversink between them. These 500 acres of publicly-owned land represent less than half the acreage of Neversink Mountain. The majority of the remainder, mainly on the south face, is owned by several large businesses, including Empire Wrecking, First Energy (Met Ed), and Forest Hills Cemetery. The rest is held by private interests, including some homeowners.

The intent of the Conservancy is to turn its Neversink land holdings over to The County of Berks, a complicated process involving trusts, banks, and politics. The goal is the creation of a public park on the mountain, with hiking and bicycling trails which can be used by future generations.

In the meantime, hikers are cautioned to respect the private property rights of the current owners in their travels on Neversink. The Conservancy occasionally offers guided hikes on the mountain, and this is the best way to become familiar with which areas are "open to the public" and which are not.

The mountain is a very valuable resource, with a rich and interesting history. Until now, that history has been scattered in many places, including the minds of surviving "old timers."

This book has endeavored not to glorify past development of Neversink, but rather to identify artifacts that may still be found, and to preserve the history of Neversink for future generations.

Hopefully, in turn, future generations will endeavor to preserve the mountain as a resource for all Berks Countians to enjoy. Unlike the motorcycle hill climbs of the 1940s and 50s, it is hoped that these uses will be appropriate, and to the benefit of Neversink Mountain as a natural resource.

Lovers of Antietam Lake and Mt. Penn know that Neversink is not the only natural resource in Berks that needs protection and preservation. But none of these resources will be protected if the people who love them remain silent. Tell the County Commissioners you want a "Neversink Park." Your grandchildren deserve it.

Top: One of the excursion steamboats which serviced the Schuylkill during the early days of the resort period. The dock was between Klapperthal Station and the power house.
(Paul Druzba)
Bottom: Tickets for Johnny Hiester's steamboat rides on the Schuylkill. Note various spellings of "Clapperthal".
(Meiser: Echoes of Scholla)

A mineral water bottle, complete with metal stopper, from the White House Bottling Works, when JL Lawrence was the proprietor. About 1900. (Druzba)

Acknowledgments

The past would be lost forever if not for the efforts of those who devote themselves to its recording and preservation. So I'm indebted to the following people (living or late) for their record-keeping and personal insights.

George M. Meiser IX and Gloria Jean Meiser, for their painstaking efforts over many years in compiling "The Passing Scene" volumes (currently 12 in number, 13 in the works).

Earl Lincoln Ruppert, late Exeter Township historian

Morton L. Montgomery and Francis W. Balthaser, late Berks historians

Stan Bakenstoss, an Exeter Township high school teacher who takes students on hikes on Neversink and keeps the history alive.

Frank Suchomelly of Exeter Township and his wife Cora, who lived through part of this narrative and shared their memories.

Bob Bartmann and the Berks County Conservancy, who have done a lot to preserve Neversink Mountain, not only for its history, but also as a natural resource for future generations.

Stan Walters, a 100 year old, who was living on the slopes of Neversink in 2002, and remembered early life on the mountain.

Vallie Reich, an extraordinary volunteer at the Reading Public Library main branch in Reading, whose help was immeasurable.

Anna Moyer Wert, sister of Vallie Reich. Provided valuable insight into what life was like at the Neversink Sanatorium.

Freeman Pauley, who was 82 and living on Klapperthal Road in 2002, and gave valuable insight into the early years of Neversink.

Carl Drobek Jr., who remembered life on Neversink in the 1930s as if it were yesterday.

Katy Jean May, a graphic artist, children's book illustrator, and my daughter, who designed the front and back covers for this book. She also designed the covers for the video, "Berks County: The First 250 Years." Thanks, KJ.

And my wife Wanda, who spent untold hours with computer and cassette, transcribing interviews for this book. God bless her.

As this is my first venture into publishing, credit must be given for insight and advice from the Historical Society of Berks County, and from Charles J. Adams III.

About The Author

Paul A. Druzba, a native of Berks County (specifically, East Reading), is the author and producer of "Berks County: The First 250 Years," a history video which was designed to be a teaching tool in the schools of Berks County. The video may still be available at the Historical Society of Berks County.

He has also written numerous historical articles for "The WEEU Journal," formerly "The Feedback Journal"- an annual publication of his employer, WEEU Radio in Reading.

Druzba is an avid collector of old postcards and memorabilia of Reading and Berks County, which provided some of the illustrations for this book. He also served as a volunteer in Public Relations for the 250th anniversaries of the City of Reading in 1998, and Berks County in 2002.

He is also a card-carrying member of the Historical Society of Berks County, The Berks County Conservancy, and the Berks County Public Library System, and encourages you to do the same.

Sources

"The Passing Scene," volumes 1 through 12, by George M. Meiser IX and Gloria Jean Meiser. This painstaking effort began as a collection of articles which appeared in the Reading Eagle in the 1960s and 1970s, and continues as an invaluable record of life and times in Berks County up to the present.

The Reading Eagle (and the former Reading Times), which are available on microfilm at the Reading Public Library, back to the Eagle's founding in 1868.

"History of Reading and Sesquicentennial" by Morton L. Montgomery, 1898, a souvenir book of the 150th anniversary of Reading.

"Sights and Sounds of the Past," an article by Earl L. Ruppert, from "Exeter, The Forgotten Corner: 225th Anniversary," a commemorative booklet produced in 1966.

"Echoes of Scholla- Illustrated" by Arthur D. Graeff and George M. Meiser IX, 1976, produced from accounts of Mr. Graeff which appeared in the Reading Times and Eagle. This volume, part of a quartet of publications issued by the "Berksiana Foundation", is an underrated treasure trove of local history.

"The History of Berks County" by Morton L. Montgomery, two volumes, 1909, which is now available in CD-rom format, fully searchable.

"The Story of Berks County" by Francis W. Balthaser, 1925, which was lovingly reproduced by the Historical Society of Berks County in honor of the county's 250th anniversary in 2002, and is now sold out.

"The Neversink Item," a "company" publication by the Neversink Mountain Railroad interests, published during the railway's early years.

"A Short History of the Neversink Mountain Railroad," from a series called "Fact and Fancy" by Bruce A. Hoffman, the acknowledged "official historian of Birdsboro."

Personal interviews with Frank Suchomelly, Stan Bakenstoss, Stan Walters, Carl Drobek Jr., Freeman Pauley and Anna Moyer Wert.

"Neversink Mountain and Its Railroad" by Albert Green. This is an eight-page recollection of the history of Neversink, recounted to and compiled by his son James in 1971-72. Some errors, but lots of useful information. This has not been published, and is only available publicly at the Historical Society of Berks County.

"The Berks and Schuylkill Journal," a weekly publication that is available on microfilm at the Historical Society of Berks County library.

"The Trolleys of Berks County" by Harry Foesig, published in 1970. A meticulous and accurate account.

The "Historical Review of Berks County"- the seasonal publication of the Historical Society of Berks County, which contains a wealth of articles on a wide range of historical topics concerning Berks. It's available, in bound editions dating back to the 1960s, at the Reading Public Library, where an index to all editions is available. The Review is delivered as part of your membership in the Historical Society.

"Handy Reference Railway Guide," a publication of the Reading Electric trolley companies, 1902.

"Reading: It's Representative Business Men and Its Points of Interest," published by Mercantile Illustrating Company, New York. 1893.

Annual Reports of the Water Board of Reading- dry reading, to be sure, but for the history buff looking for factual information, a gold mine. Available at the Historical Society.

"Dickon Among the Lenape Indians", M.R. Harrington, Chicago, 1938.

Illustrations, as noted in the text, from various publications, as well as from the personal collections of George M. Meiser IX, Vallie Reich, Anna Moyer Wert, Corrie Crupi, Frank Suchomelly, and the author.
Cover illustrations: Front- Meiser/Passing Scene. Back: Druzba